# International Trade
# in Textiles

# International Trade in Textiles

## MFA Quotas and a Developing Exporting Country

## SRI RAM KHANNA

**Sage Publications**
New Delhi/Newbury Park/London

To my late father, Suraj Prakash Khanna, and my mother, Sheela Khanna

*First published in 1991 by*

**Sage Publications India Pvt Ltd**
**M-32 Greater Kailash Market I**
**New Delhi 110 048**

**Sage Publications Inc**
2455 Teller Road
Newbury Park, California 91320

**Sage Publications Ltd**
6 Bonhill Street
London EC2A 4PU

Published by Tejeshwar Singh for Sage Publications India Pvt Ltd, phototypeset by
Jayigee Enterprises, and printed at Chaman Enterprises, Delhi.

**Library of Congress Cataloging-in-Publication Data**

Khanna, Sri Ram.
    International trade in textiles : MFA quotas and a developing
export country/Sriram Khanna.
    p.    cm.
Includes bibliographical references and index.
    1. Textile industry—India. I. Title.
HD9866.I62K45    1991    382'.45677'00954—dc20    91-3465

**ISBN** : 81-7036-234-2 (India)
        0-8039-9690-X (US)

# Contents

# List of Tables

# Foreword

One of the early signatories to the MFA, India is among the major suppliers of apparels and textiles to developed markets. In recent years apparel exports have assumed greater significance as an important earner of foreign exchange for the country. MFA's binding restrictions have outlived their utility even from the point of view of importing countries. Their indefinite continuance hampers international trade and hurts industry. There are few studies on the impact of MFA quota restrictions (QRs) on the economies of developing exporting countries. The present study seeks to fill this gap in the literature on India and MFA regulations.

Dr. Khanna, author of this innovative study, defines the nature of QRs and unravels their implications for corporate policy makers and behaviour of apparel exporting firms. This is sought to be achieved by testing a set of hypotheses in the introductory chapter. In the succeeding chapters, the impact of multi-fibre arrangements on the apparel industry in India is examined, and the adverse consequences for the country's export income are analysed.

To supplement and support his findings, the author has assembled detailed data on almost every aspect of this industry. In Part I attention has been focused on the composition of India's apparel exports, the utilisation of quotas, working of the quota system, quota rents, export prices and our comparative advantage. In Part II, the attitudes, views, and reactions of apparel exporting firms on interconnected issues are discussed. In the concluding chapter an attempt is made to delineate future directions for the expansion of the apparel exports industry.

The multi-fibre arrangements have been extended four times, notwithstanding the opposition of LDCs, including India and Brazil.

It is to be hoped that the international community will soon evolve a consensus on phasing out these arrangements. It is important that in the meanwhile India's apparel industry builds on its comparative advantage and strengthens its competitive capability. It is prudent on their part to embark on internationalising their operations.

Government policy is expected to aim at providing facilities for improvement of quality and incentives for trade-related investments and strategic alliances.

I have pleasure in commending this study to the attention of all those in administration, business, and industry, in India and abroad, who are interested in accelerating the development of the apparel industry and augmenting the country's export income.

K.B. LALL
**Chairman**

Indian Council for Research on
International Economic Relations
40 Lodi Estate
New Delhi-110003.
7 November 1990.

# Preface

The new-protectionism in the developed market economies in the form of a wide variety of non-tariff barriers (NTBs) to exports of manufactures and semi-manufactures from developing countries has become a major cause of concern. International trade in apparel and textiles is a sector which exhibits this new-protectionism in an institutionalised form. MFA is the multilateral agreement which accords legitimacy to such a regime. This agreement is grossly discriminatory to interests of LDCs, particularly cotton growing countries, small suppliers and least developed countries who are not being allowed to export apparel and textiles on a scale commensurate with their needs. Moreover, MFA which has been in force since 1974 has been once more extended in 1986 to run a fourth term till 1991. India is one of the signatories to the MFA and is also a marginal supplier of apparel and textiles to developed markets. In recent years apparel exports have assumed greater importance than non-apparel textile exports as foreign exchange earners for India. As a result of expansion of exports, during MFA-III many items of Indian apparel exports became subject to binding restrictions under MFA. While there is considerable understanding about the impact of MFA restrictions on the economies of importing countries, there have been few studies on the impact of MFA quotas on the exporting country. The present study seeks to fill this gap.

The Indian Council for Research in International Economic Relations (ICRIER) extended its sponsorship and support to the study. Dr. K.B. Lall, Chairman, ICRIER motivated me to begin work on its predecessor link study—"Impact of QRs on India's Apparel Industry (1987)" and has also been a source of inspiration to this work. I acknowledge with appreciation the encouragement given by Prof. Charan Wadhwa to continue my work in this area. I am deeply indebted to a number of institutions and individuals who have assisted me in different ways. I would be failing in my duty if I do not acknowledge the valuable comments and advice received by me from Prof. Carl Hamilton, and two experts who gave their comments on a blind review of the mid-term report. I would also like to mention the suggestions and advice given by Dr. Martin Wolf, Dr. Vincent Cable, Prof. Jose De La Torre, Prof. Brian Toyne, Dr. T.S. Chen, Shri H.F. Lau, Prof. V.R. Panchmukhi, Dr. Rajiv Kumar, Dr. Pronab Sen, Dr. S. Bhashyam, Dr. S.K. Jain, and Shri Sanjay Kathuria.

The secondary data used was obtained from the Apparel Export Promotion Council (AEPC) to whose support I am deeply indebted. Mr. Sidharth Rajgopal, Mr. Reddy and Mr. Raju of AEPC always responded favourably to my requests for data and clarifications. For the primary data I must record my deep appreciation for the top management of 177 enterprises who cooperated during lengthy interviews and repeated visits. The names of these enterprises are being kept confidential at their request. I must also accord my acknowledgement of the cooperation extended by the Garment Exporters Association (GEA), Apparel Exporters and Manufacturers Association (AEMA) and Clothing Manufacturers Association of India (CMAI) during this study.

The most exacting part of the study was primary data collection. The mail response to questionnaires was only 0.04% and considerable effort had to be undertaken to collect data from 177 enterprises in Delhi, Bombay and Madras. I am indebted to Mr. R.N. Sharma and Mr. V.R. Raghu, the AEPC officers at Bombay and Madras respectively, who assisted in arranging interviews with respondents. I am also grateful to my PGDIM students at Delhi School of Economics who volunteered to assist me in data collection, its processing and proof-reading at different phases of the study. I am particularly indebted to Mr. Rajesh Dudeja for his assistance in completing the project and to Siby Mathew for proof-reading the typescript. I gratefully acknowledge the support and facilities extended by the University of Delhi and Prof. R.K. Lele, Head, Deptt. of Commerce, Delhi School of Economics.

I am indeed grateful to my family for its wholehearted support to my work on this project. My wife Radhika was a constant source of encouragement throughout the course of the study.

SRI RAM KHANNA

# Introduction

Quantitative restrictions in the form of MFA quotas (also referred to as Voluntary Export Restraints or VERs) have affected the exports of the Indian apparel industry. Indian exports of apparel (i.e.; readymade garments) rose from Rs. 125 million in 1970–71 to Rs. 10,676 million in 1985, Rs. 18,570 million in 1987 and have crossed Rs. 43,775.6 million in 1990 at current prices. Though the growth has been phenomenal, its quantum has been seriously affected by quota restrictions particularly in the US, Canadian and Swedish markets. These quota restrictions are administered by the Apparel Export Promotion Council through a yearly quota distribution policy. Within the constraints of annual levels this quota policy allocates the intra-industry distribution of annual levels among exporting firms.

The inception and growth of the Indian apparel industry were almost entirely the result of external demand. Apparel exports were only Rs. 63.8 million in 1965–66 at which time there were only about 100 garment-exporting firms registered with the Textile Export Promotion Council. By 1970–71 apparel exports had risen to Rs. 125 million. There was a phenomenal growth between 1970 and 1977 and exports reached Rs. 2,625.5 million in 1976–77. By this time the number of apparel-exporting firms was nearing 4,000. It was around this time that the Apparel Export Promotion Council was set up by the Indian government to initiate organised export promotion for this industry. This growth in Indian apparel exports to Western Europe and North American markets in the early 1970s was perceived as causing some degree of market disruption which, in turn, led to the imposition of quantitative restrictions (QRs) on Indian exports to these markets. These QRs continue till today.

Textile and apparel exports together constitute about one-fifth of

India's total exports—apparel exports alone account for more than one-eighth of the total. Table 1 shows the increase in the percentage of apparel exports as a share of total Indian exports—from over 6 per cent to almost 13 per cent during the last few years. However, these rising exports are insufficient to overcome chronic trade deficits that have become a permanent feature of India's foreign trade. The overall trade deficit during 1987–88 stood at Rs. 66.2 billion ($ 509.5 million)—about 12 per cent less than the deficit of Rs. 75.1 billion during 1986–87. However, despite gains which look impressive at home, India remains a marginal supplier to major world markets. India's share in the volume of extra-EC imports has remained at about 3.5 per cent since 1978. Its value share in extra-EC imports has declined from 4 per cent in 1978 to 3.7 per cent in 1986. The Indian share of exports of textiles and apparel to the US was only 3.3 per cent in 1987, having risen marginally from 2.5 per cent in 1985.

Apart from 1982, apparel exports have been rising steadily since the mid-1960s. Table 2 shows the steady growth of India's apparel exports both in terms of value and volume. India's apparel exports suffered a brief setback during 1982 and 1983 due to a decrease in exports to EC countries. Exports to the EC have, however, accelerated steadily since 1984, with a sharp rise during 1987. Informed trade sources attributed the setback of 1982 and 1983 partly to a 'not so hot' summer, accompanied by a fashion swing. However, the particularly sharp rise in exports to the EC during 1987 is attributed in part to India's exchange rate policy of allowing the rupee to fall with the US dollar, leading to a fall in the value of the rupee against major European currencies and resulting in enhanced competitiveness of Indian exports in EC markets. Export growth to the EC, however, levelled off during 1988 rising only 16 per cent by rupee value and declining 0.9 per cent by volume. This indicates that volume growth is becoming restricted due to quota ceilings in the EC.

Indian garments were exported to 125 countries during 1985. Of total exports of Rs. 10,676.5 million (255.9 million pieces) 97.4 per cent by value and 96.8 per cent by volume were accounted for by only twenty-one countries. Of these, sixteen imposed quantitative restrictions, one country imposed a global tariff-quota (Australia) and two countries (Japan and Switzerland) used other non-tariff barriers. Two were centrally planned economies—the USSR imposed limits under bilateral trade plans while Hungary administered imports. The remaining 104 countries accounted for only 2.6 and

Table 1

Share of Apparel and Textiles in India's Total Exports, 1983–84 to 1988–89

| | 1983–84 | | 1984–85 | | 1985–86 | | 1987–88 | | 1988–89 | |
|---|---|---|---|---|---|---|---|---|---|---|
| | Value (Rs. mn) | Share (%) | Value (Rs. mn) | Share (%) | Value (Rs. mn) | Share (%) | Value (Rs. mn) | Share (%) | Value (Rs. mn) | Share (%) |
| Apparel[a] | 6,072 | 6.15 | 8,373 | 7.28 | 15,090 | 12.0 | 20,250 | 12.88 | 23,119 | 11.4 |
| Textiles, made-ups and yarns[b] | 4,395 | 4.45 | 5,957 | 5.18 | 7,846 | 6.24 | 16,386 | 10.4 | 19,288 | 9.51 |
| All exports[c] | 98,721 | 100.00 | 114,937.2 | 100.0 | 125,666.0 | 100.0 | 157,194 | 100.0 | 202,810 | 100.0 |

Source : a : AEPC Statistical Reports (various issues), New Delhi.
b : Ministry of Textiles, Government of India, New Delhi.
c : Ministry of Commerce, Government of India, New Delhi.

Note : Average exchange rates: $1 = Rs. 10.099 in 1983, Rs. 11.363 in 1984, Rs. 12.369 in 1985, Rs. 12.611 in 1986, Rs. 12.962 in 1987 and Rs. 13.043 in the first quarter of 1988.

Table 2

*Indian Apparel Exports*

| Year | No.of Export Firms | Value | | Volume | |
|---|---|---|---|---|---|
| | | *(Rs million)* | *% Change* | *(million pieces)* | *% change* |
| 1965–66 | 120 | 63.8 | – | n.a. | – |
| 1976–77 | 3923 | 2,625.5 | – | n.a. | – |
| 1980 | n.a. | 4,534.9 | – | 141.3 | – |
| 1981 | n.a. | 6,500.2 | 43.3 | 199.0 | 40.8 |
| 1982 | n.a. | 6,335.7 | –2.5 | 187.0 | –6.0 |
| 1983 | 4173 | 6,401.3 | 1.0 | 193.4 | 3.4 |
| 1984 | 4715 | 8,501.0 | 32.8 | 230.5 | 19.2 |
| 1985 | n.a. | 10,676.5 | 25.5 | 255.9 | 11.0 |
| 1986 | 8262* | 13,231.2 | 23.9 | 300.8 | 17.7 |
| 1987 | 11149† | 18,574.3 | 40.4 | 384.2 | 27.7 |
| 1988 | ††n.a. | 21,486.4 | 15.7 | 396.7 | 3.2 |
| 1989 | 13346 | 31,182.1 | 45.1 | 498.4 | 25.6 |
| 1990 | 17546 | 43,775.6 | 41.6 | 602.7 | 22.0 |

Source : 1. Apparel Export Promotion Council, New Delhi.
2. Rajya Sabha unstarred question No. 220 dated 19 November, 1985.
3. S.R. Khanna, 1985.
Note : * As on April 1986.
† As on 30 June 1988.
†† As on 31 July 1990.

3.2 per cent of the total value and volume, respectively, of Indian apparel exports in 1985. During 1988 these twenty-one countries accounted for 95.8 per cent by value and 93.3 per cent by volume of India's total apparel exports. This pattern of apparel export destinations has remained substantially the same throughout the 1980s.

Indian exports have been directed to two groups of markets over the period under study. The first group consists of the western MFA signatories—the USA, the EC (excluding Spain and Portugal), Norway, Sweden, Finland, Austria and Canada. These sixteen quota countries accounted for 73.2 per cent by value (75.4 per cent by volume) of India's apparel exports during 1985, having fluctuated between 65.8 per cent and 81.6 per cent during the first half of the decade. The largest markets within these quota countries are the USA and the EC—both being the major partners in the MFA. The other group, consisting of the remaining five countries, accounted for only 24.2 per cent by value (21.4 per cent by volume) in 1985. Changes in quotas, therefore, had an impact on the great bulk of India's total apparel exports.

During 1985, 64.09 per cent of Indian exports to sixteen quota countries consisted of five primary apparel products, namely: blouses, shirts, ladies' dresses, skirts, and trousers. Table 16 shows the volume and value share of these five products as a percentage of all exports by the Indian garment industry.

The share of primary products remains high despite a marginal decline over the period, signifying a narrow range of product specialisation for the country as a whole. This specialisation becomes even narrower at the level of the firm, given the large number of small export firms in India.

## SCOPE OF THE STUDY

The main objective of this study is to investigate the nature of the impact of QRs on the corporate policy behaviour of the apparel exporting firms. These objectives were sought to be achieved by testing the following hypotheses:

1. Underutilised quotas may also restrict trade.
2. Over-categorisation acts as a restriction intensifier to enhance the trade restrictive effects of quotas.
3. Quotas induce quota cornering activity among firms in the exporting country.
4. In respect of trade subject to QRs, quota rents in the exporting country occur in only those product categories exported to a specific country where restrictions actually become binding at the export firm level.
5. Under a quota regime export firms generally tend to decentralise production operations due to dis-economies of centralisation.
6. Marketing strategy of firms shifts from restrained categories/countries to quota free markets/products.
7. Quotas have adversely affected the employment in the Indian apparel industry.
8. Quotas have adversely affected growth of real investment in the Indian apparel industry.
9. Quotas tend to enhance market and/or product diversification among export firms.
10. Large-sized firms are more successful in maintaining their sales under a quota regime.

11. Highly export oriented firms are more successful in maintaining their sales under a quota regime.

Hypotheses nos. 1 to 4 are being answered positively on the basis of analysis of secondary data maintained by the Apparel Export Promotion Council (AEPC), New Delhi, in Part I of this study.

Hypotheses nos. 5 to 11 which relate directly to the behavioural response of export firms were tested in the first phase of the present study on the basis of a sample of eighty-five firms in Delhi, Bombay and Madras. Findings of this survey were presented in the form of a preliminary report in 1987. It was felt that the sample of firms in the first phase of the study was too small and the findings needed to be validated from a larger sample. Consequently, the second phase of the survey was conducted in late 1987 using an abridged questionnaire. Another ninety-two firms were interviewed and the combined data base from 177 responding firms has been used. The findings relating to hypotheses 5 to 11 are presented in Part II of this study.

# PART I

## MULTI-FIBRE ARRANGEMENT AND APPAREL QUOTAS

# 1

# Multi-Fibre Arrangement: Past and Future

The Multi-Fibre Arrangement has been extended for a further term of five years under a protocol that became effective on 1 August 1986. Though scheduled to expire in July 1991, it is likely to roll over due to the breakdown of the Uruguay Round of GATT talks where an agreement to phase out the MFA is being negotiated. The Multi-Fibre Agreement (MFA) negotiated in December 1981 for a third tenure of four and a half years ended on 31 July 1986. MFA-I was negotiated by some fifty governments in the final months of 1973 and lasted from 1 January 1974 to the end of 1977. MFA-II was negotiated in December 1977 and ran a full term of four years, till the end of 1981.

## BEFORE THE MFA

MFA-I did not emerge as an innovation of international diplomacy. It was the natural consequence of the developments in global trade in textiles after the second world war. The liberal and non-discriminatory rules of international trade enshrined in the GATT were never applied to the field of cotton textiles from the very beginning. There was a slow growth in the demand for products of the cotton textile industries of the developed countries in the post-war years. It was accompanied by autonomous shifts in comparative advantage towards the cotton textile industries of developing countries. Japan and Hong Kong appeared as the pioneers in textile exports in the post-war years followed by South Korea and Taiwan emerging as significant exporters during the 1960s (Keesing and Wolf, 1980). The size of the textile industry of the west in terms of turnover and employment was large and its political lobby strong. The developing countries maintained a low profile under the GATT trading system at the time when developed countries sought to institutionalise protectionism in the textile trade. The first sign of institutionalised protectionism appeared in the form of the 'Short Term Arrangement' (STA) of July 1961 regulating imports of cotton textiles. The STA was soon replaced by the 'Long Term Arrangement' (LTA) in February 1962. This was designed to prevent the rapid penetration of imported textiles in the developed markets with a view to avoiding serious injury or threat thereof to domestic producers. The developed countries were already violating Articles I and XIX of GATT by taking discriminatory action and sought a multilateral agreement on exceptions to the GATT rules.

The geopolitical framework following the allied victory in the second world war that provided the global economic environment for the creation of the General Agreement on Tariffs and Trade (GATT) has changed significantly as we approach the final decade of this century. The victorious allied states were in a benevolent mood and sought to establish principles of non-discrimination among states entering into international trade. However, the fires of protectionism were first to erupt in the late 1950s as Japanese textile exports began to penetrate the US market. Domestic pressure for restricting Japanese textile imports to the USA arose mainly from the US textile regions of Maine, South Carolina, Alabama, Georgia, Louisiana, Mississippi and Massachusets which organised state government action against Japanese textiles as well as boycott at local levels. As the first US Senate motion to impose quotas on import of textiles was lost by only two votes on 28 June 1956, the US federal administration began looking for ways and means to curb these imports without jeopardising US obligations under GATT. The US successfully applied political pressure to make the post-war Japanese government agree to Voluntary Export Restraints (VERs) on textiles. The US and West European concerns and honour for GATT were sensitive in this geopolitical framework which produced the first VER mechanism. The Japanese VERs also stimulated enquiries from other states such as West Germany and Canada. However, as other exporting states such as Hong Kong refused to agree to VERs, the US administration under President Eisenhower sought means to legalise such VERs as GATT rules did not allow it. The legalisation of VERs and institutionalisation of protectionism emerged in the form of the Short Term Arrangement (STA) on cotton textiles. The terms of US presidents J.F. Kennedy and L.B. Johnson saw the extension of this framework under the Long Term Arrangement.

The LTA quotas could be imposed unilaterally but quota levels could not be lower than actual imports in the preceding 12 months period. These quotas were allowed a 5 per cent annual growth but lower growth rates could be agreed mutually. The LTA was limited to cotton textiles as at the relevant time western textile industries perceived a threat only from the cotton textile imports from low wage countries.

The 12-year term of LTA witnessed growth in exports of textile products from LDCs particularly due to changing trends in consumer preferences for non-cotton fibres. LDC textile and clothing industries sought to overcome LTA controls by switching to man-made fibre (regenerated as well as synthetic) products which remained outside the LTA. Western textile industries witnessed a fall in employment over this period. Even where western textile industries could enhance their competitiveness due to innovation and technological development, the apparel industry remained a labour intensive production function. Developments in transportation and communication added to the competitiveness of several LDC apparel industries. South Korea, Taiwan and Hong Kong emerged as the Big-3 apparel exporters over this period.

USA was among the leading advocates of protectionism as it imposed restrictions on non-LTA textile products from Japan, Taiwan, South Korea and Hong Kong in 1971. The first MFA was negotiated in 1973 under American advocacy and implemented with effect from 1 January 1974. Thus the effort to bring imports of non-cotton textile products under control succeeded with the signing of MFA-I.

## MFA-I

The US administration had been under severe pressure to widen the scope of VERs to include wool and synthetic textiles as well. This pressure was resisted until the Nixon presidency. Nixon pledged to widen the scope of textile protection in exchange for the support of the US textile lobby for his 1968 election compaign (Yoffie, 1983: 131). The major exporters at that time included East Asian states of Japan, Taiwan, Hong Kong and South Korea, all of whom soon succumbed to political, diplomatic and economic pressures of the US and signed bilateral agreements by 15 October 1971. With major exporting nations now towing the line, the MFA was formally negotiated as an agreed departure from GATT rules to allow for a comprehensive and sophisticated framework for protectionism vis-a-vis the trade in textiles. The urge for such a framework had, and continues to have, its roots in the domestic pressure from the highly organised US textile lobby in the Senate as well the Congress. This lobby has been instrumental in activising successive US administrations to renew the MFA four times since 1974—to the current MFA-IV which expires in July 1991 (Giesse and Lewin, 1987: 88).

MFA-I was the result of a forced consensus between unequal trading partners. The governments of developed countries, backed by their respective domestic textile lobbies, were eager to postpone the consequences of the autonomous shifts in comparative advantages in favour of low wage developing countries. The LTA had been envisaged as a 'temporary' measure and had been extended from time to time to complete a twelve year term. MFA-I that followed it was even more drastic in its future implications as it represented three basic features:

1. That international trade in all types of textiles and apparels was somehow a special case in itself and did not justify applicability of the non-discriminatory principles of GATT.
2. That discriminatory restrictions on exports of textiles and apparels from particular LDC sources were valid instruments for protecting the textile and apparel industries of the west.
3. That actual or threatened disruption of the domestic markets of importing countries due to imports of particular products from particular sources was necessary for protecting their textile and clothing industries.

MFA-I at its core was an instrument of forced consensus designed to manage textile trade to the advantage of countries that were fast losing international competitiveness in these lines of production. It built up an elaborate regime for managing trade in order to avoid disruptive effects in individual markets and on individual lines of production in both importing and exporting countries (see MFA-I text: page 2). This agreement also aimed at furthering 'The economic and social development of developing countries and secure a substantial increase in their export earnings from textile products and to provide for a greater share for them in world trade in these products' (see MFA-I text: article I, para 3). In retrospect it can be stated that far from achieving this aim, MFA-I set the tone for achieving exactly the opposite.

Based on artificial consensus, this multilateral 'treaty' knit an elaborate system of procedures for implementing its objective. The following were its main features:

1. All parties agreed to apply safeguard measures only in 'exceptional' circumstances and in accordance with the manner in which this treaty allowed (see MFA-I text: article 1, para 5).
2. Under article 3, importing countries could apply safeguard measures only when market disruption was being caused in terms of the specific definitions enshrined in Annex A to the agreement. The determination of a situation of 'market disruption' was based on the existence of serious damage to domestic producers or actual threat thereof. The damage had to exist in terms of actual (or imminent) sharp, substantial and measurable increase in imports of particular products from particular sources. The damage was also contemplated in terms of low price of the imported goods in relation to similar goods of comparable quality in the market of the importing country.
3. The importing country would seek consultation with the exporting country indicating the level at which it would like to restrain such exports. The restraint levels could not be lower than actual exports during the twelve month period preceding the consultations.
4. For products for which restraint levels have been specified a growth rate of 6 per cent per annum was generally allowed except in cases where such growth would worsen the disruption. In such cases a lower but positive growth rate could be decided by consultation.
5. It envisaged the setting up of a Textiles Surveillance Body (TSB) to examine disputes and make recommendations to the

Textiles Committee of GATT. However, these were not necessarily binding.

6. Article 4 enabled conclusion of bilateral agreements between importing and exporting countries within the overall framework of MFA-I.

7. The administration of the quotas set under articles 3 and 4 should be so as to facilitate full utilisation of such quotas among exporters.

8. The coverage of product items was widened to include tops, yarns, piece goods, made-ups, apparels of cotton, wool, man-made fibres or blends thereof. However, article 12 (para 3) exempted handloom fabrics of developing countries or hand-made cottage industry products made from handloom fabrics. The exemption granted to such products, however, came to face problems in the later years.

## MFA - II

MFA-II came into force on 1 January 1978 as a result of a protocol signed on 14 December 1977. The participating countries agreed to renew the MFA for a second term on the basis of the conclusions of the Textiles Committee of GATT about the working of MFA-I.

In the protocol of extensions it was stated that there had been several difficulties in the implementation of provisions of MFA-I both for importing countries as well as exporting countries. Yet world trade in textiles needed to be satisfactorily managed in the interest of the importing as well as exporting countries. Despite these difficulties the participating countries agreed to renew the arrangement. The participants agreed to resolve the problems bilaterally within the framework of the MFA whenever problems arose.

The major change in MFA-II was that a 'reasonable departures' clause was introduced. Under this clause trading partners could mutually agree to depart from the general terms of the MFA in particular elements in particular cases. This was nothing but an escape clause for participants who found themselves in difficult situations. These 'departures' were to be temporary and participants were obliged to return to the framework of the MFA 'in the shortest possible time'. Yet these departures once made tended to be of a continuing nature. In retrospect it can be stated that this clause served the purpose of strong protectionist sentiments within importing countries.

This clause limited the expansion of LDC imports into developed countries thus making MFA-II more restrictive than MFA-I. The reasons for this result were not far to seek. During 1974–78, 0.34 million jobs were lost in the textile sector in nine member-states of EEC. Between 1973 and 1976 the volume of imports from MFA participants rose by 80 per cent and the EEC alone absorbed 72 per cent of the increase in world textile imports between 1973 and 1975. The reasonable departures clause allowed less than 6 per cent growth rates in annual levels. The EEC set internal global ceilings for eight ultra-sensitive products which were to be allowed a growth rate of only 1 to 2 per cent per annum. Sensitive items in Group II were to be allowed up to 4 per cent growth while others could increase at 6 per cent (Englert, *The International Trade in Textiles*). In almost every bilateral agreement negotiated by the EEC under MFA-II the 'reasonable departures' clause was used to cut growth rates.

The MFA-II akin to its predecessor paid lip service to developing countries. The reiteration that 'the special problems of developing countries shall be fully taken into account in a manner consistent with the provisions of the MFA' (see para 8 conclusion in MFA-II never came to be realised during the second MFA.

## MFA - III

The third MFA (January 1982–July 1986) was negotiated in an atmosphere of increasing concern among developing countries as to the undesirable impact on their exports in the past. In the first few months of 1981 alone the EEC brought in over thirty-three restrictions following the triggering off a device known as the 'basket extractor mechanism'.[1] Seven of these restrictions concerned China while

---

[1] The EEC policy includes a 'basket extractor mechanism' based on the concept of cumulative market disruption where there is an absoloute limit on market penetration from 'low cost' sources. Under this mechanism when non-restrained imports reach a certain percentage of EEC imports in the preceding year from all sources in that category, a trigger in the mechanism goes off . The EEC can make consultation calls and fix a quota even for such a non-quota category. Under article 8 of the current Indo-EEC bilateral agreement effective till 1991, the mechanism triggers off when

three concerned India. The severity of these restrictions during MFA-II led to quota frauds wherein exporters in LDCs, where quotas had been exhausted, rerouted their exports through third countries or under different product categories. According to the European Commission the biggest of such frauds involved South Korea during 1978 and 1979. Korea agreed to the partial offsetting of these exports against 1981 quotas (Englert, *The International Trade in Textiles*).

In a study that was released shortly before the conclusion of MFA-III it was stated that the newer suppliers among LDCs were the worst sufferers of MFA. The report stated:

> It is the newer suppliers, however, who are hardly being allowed to attempt textiles and clothing exports on a scale commensurate with their needs and potential. It is disingenuous, therefore, to argue that the large suppliers are being cut back in favour of the smaller ones, when it remains the case that the former enjoys by far the larger quotas and more vital still—the latter will not be permitted within the current framework any comparable export gains (Keesing and Wolf, 1980: 165).

At the conference table in 1981, the EEC's stand was the most protectionist of all. The EEC found itself totally isolated as Japan, Sweden and USA took up positions which were far less restrictive. The initial US proposals were considered very positive by the LDCs. However, just a week before the signing of the extension protocol on 22 December 1981, the US delegation reversed their liberal position and made a volte face to the EEC position. 'The US politicians linked to the textile lobby had made their approval of the budget dependent on their demands for protection to the textile market,' (Englert, *The International Trade in Textiles*).

The conclusion of the Textiles Committee which provided a basis for MFA-III carried the following notable features:

1. Safeguard measures would be invoked by importers only if there was market disruption or risk thereof due to imports.

---

the Indian exports of a non-restrained category to EEC reach a level of 1 per cent of global imports into EEC in case of Group I (ultra-sensitive) products, 5 per cent for Group II (sensitive) products and 10 per cent in Group III (non-sensitive) products.

Such market disruption as defined in Annex A had led to mis-understandings during MFA-II. The participants reiterated that disciplines of Annex A and procedures of articles 3 and 4 would be fully adhered to in the future. In this respect requests for action should be accompanied by relevant factual information on specific items.

2. It agreed to cutbacks in the form of lower positive growth rates in case of recurrence or exacerbation of market disruption. Such cutbacks would be agreed to bilaterally particularly in respect of large suppliers. It also provided for 'compensation' to suppliers affected by such action.

3. It also agreed to bilateral solutions being found for problems of market disruption in countries having small markets (i.e., Nordic countries), an exceptionally high level of imports, a correspondingly low level of production. Such solutions were justified on grounds of avoidance of damage to 'minimum viable' production of textiles in such countries.

4. It recognised the special problems faced by small suppliers, new entrants and cotton textile exporters. It was agreed to treat textiles and apparels separately for working out import shares and give them favourable treatments in regard to restraints.

5. It agreed to deal with problems relating to circumvention of the arrangement by mutual consultation on measures which could include adjustments that would debit the true country of origin.

6. It decided to set up a sub-committee to monitor developments in the autonomous adjustment process in the importing countries on the basis of data provided by participants to the arrangement.

With these features it became apparent that MFA-III was opening its door wide for disguised bilateralism to absorb shocks that were perceived by importing countries, particularly those in the EEC. Doors for bilateral arm twisting were wide open to evolve 'mutually acceptable arrangements' under threat of unilateral action.

It was during MFA-III that Indian bilateral agreements with importing countries became restrictive in their scope and coverage. Each bilateral agreement incorporated rigid features on category ceilings, growth rates, carryover, carryforward and swing provisions. Even where quantitative celings were not imposed there were provisions for consultations and freezing of exports in non-restrained categories. Each bilateral agreement was unique in its features depending on the perceptions of the negotiating parties about the vital trade interests of the other. While the EEC resorted to its basket extractor mechanism, USA had its overall Group II ceiling and Canada also used a Group ceiling over and above individual ceilings on sensitive product categories.

## MFA-IV AND ITS FUTURE

Over twelve years of MFA has given sufficient time to the textile industries of the west to adjust to the changing international environment. The working of this arrangement has highlighted its failures that must be kept in mind for the future. This discussion confines itself to the international trade in the apparel sector of textiles. This sector, while dependent on the textile industry for its inputs, has grown internationally as an industry distinct from the non-apparel sector. The MFA applies uniformly to both sectors as at present. The following undesirable features in the working of MFA continue as its tenure is extended to 1991

1. Discrimination
2. Low price principle
3. Unjustified Consumer Burden
4. Restriction intensifier

### Discrimination

The most undesirable feature of the MFA is the derogation from the 'MFN' clause of the GATT. The restrictions only apply to LDCs and do not apply to such exports from developed market economies. Importing countries have singled out 'low cost' suppliers as inherently disruptive. The concept of 'low cost suppliers' has led to the concept of 'cumulative market disruption'. This concept says that since the import penetration by low cost suppliers has reached a peak, disruption is caused by the cumulative impact of low cost suppliers. This concept provides the rationale for an overall limit to freeze low cost imports. However, while Annex A states that volume and price factors generally appear in combination, some importers have taken 'low price' alone as an independent proof of disruption.

Developed market economies continue to be major markets for apparel as they absorbed 74.3 per cent of world apparel exports in 1970 as compared to 79.1 per cent in 1980. It is not as if all these exports originate from developing countries alone. Intra-developed country trade is a very important segment of world apparel trade. Apparel producing developed countries exported 85.8 per cent of apparels to importing developed countries in 1970 and this figure rose to 86.1 per cent in 1980. The developed market economy countries accounted for 73.1 per cent of share in total imports of this group of countries in 1970. This share declined to 55.8 per cent in 1980. The comparative shares of developing countries in the markets of the developed market economy countries were 23.6 and 38.0 per cent in 1970 and 1980 respectively. The bulk of imports into the developed market economies still continues to be from developed countries themselves. When developed markets are important both for exporters from developed (DC) as well as developing countries (LDC), a trade regime that discriminates between DCs and LDCs needs to be dismantled at the first opportunity. Apparel exports from developed market economy countries were 51.3 per cent of world apparel exports in 1980 while this share for the LDCs and socialist countries of East Europe was 36.4 per cent and 7.5 per cent respectively (UNCTAD, 1984). That more than half the world trade in apparel should be outside the regime of MFA is a discrimination that must be ended at the earliest.

Sentiments favouring such discriminatory protection were running high in USA in the year preceding the Geneva negotiations for MFA-IV. A bill passed by the US Senate in November 1985 sought a cutback on exports from three leading exporters—Taiwan, South Korea and Hong Kong—by 30 per cent and limited textile imports from other suppliers like India, China, Japan, Pakistan, Indonesia, the Philippines, Thailand, Brazil and Singapore to levels prevalent in 1984 with 1 per cent growth, a more restrictive framework than MFA-III (Rajya Sabha, unstarred question 1707, dated 3 December 1985). It was, however, dropped later under veto power of the US President. The US administration which was unable to resist pressures from the domestic textile lobby went ahead to continue the MFA to its fourth term.

## Low Price Imports and Market Disruption

Restrictions have worsened over three successive MFA regimes on the plea that disruption has intensified. We wonder whether this is 'disruption' as defined in Annex A to the MFA. The Annex A identifies it with 'serious damage' due to low priced imports from specific sources to be determined from such factors as 'turnover, market share, profits, export performance, employment, volume of disruptive and other imports, production, utilisation of capacity, productivity and investments'. If the cause is low priced imports, it would justify safeguard action under the MFA. However, disruption due to changes in technology, productivity and consumer preferences do not call for safeguard action. However, importing countries have tended to attribute all types of disruption with imports from LDCs. There is clear evidence today that productivity changes have been responsible for more jobs lost than due to low priced imports. One study tried to investigate causes of jobs lost in six EEC countries and found that productivity increases had a negative impact which was four times the impact of net import penetration. This study concluded that even if imports had not risen further after 1970, the apparel industry in the six EEC countries would have lost an estimated 141,000 jobs in six years due to productivity changes induced by import competition (Arpan, De La Torre and Toyne, 1982).

Over the past years many dominant suppliers of apparel, including those from LDCs, have increasingly upgraded their products. Even LDC firms exporting apparel in the high price segments are subject to MFA restrictions for the only reason that they are located in 'low cost' countries. Similar restrictions continue for firms who participate in outward processing trade (OPT). OPT firms generally import textiles/cut fabrics from the importing countries and re-export them after conversion into apparel. Both the EEC and the US allow importation of OPT products for apparel on a much more liberal basis than direct imports. However, this liberal treatment is available only to traditional OPT partners such as the Mediterranean Rim and Caribbean basin countries. There is no case for applying the 'low cost' criteria to high price as well as OPT apparel exports from developing countries. It would be unfair to assume that every item of apparel from a low cost country was of a low price irrespective of the actual landed c.i.f. price. The present MFA makes this assumption. It would be fair to ask such importing countries to specify the exact cut off price for apparel which would divide imports between 'low' and 'high' priced. Imports of high priced apparel can revert to the GATT regime. There is no justification for restraints of any sort on high priced imports even from low cost sources.

## Unjustified Consumer Burden

There is now a substantial body of literature which agrees that MFA quotas result in inflation of import prices resulting in quota rents to exporters as well as importers. There are at least three causes of rising import prices—quota rents, rising cost of production and product upgradation. Quota rents are a result of these quantitative restrictions. Two studies shed important light on the measurement of the tariff equivalents of such quotas. One by Hamilton estimates the tariff equivalents on apparel imports from Hong Kong to an export destination at about 18 per cent (Hamilton, 1984). Measurement of the size of quota rents has also been examined as a part of the wider exercise in measurement of non-tariff barriers to international trade by Deardorf and Stern (Deardorf and Stern, 1985). Such quotas push up import prices and result in higher retail prices. This constitutes a burden on consumers in the importing countries.

Western textile industry lobbies are well organised and support MFA quotas. But the consumer interests, on the other hand, are unorganised and are unable to influence the policy-makers to lessen the consumer burden resulting from the MFA. Ultimately, consumers in the developed economies pay the price. Hamilton calculated import tariff equivalents of quotas and found that Sweden's combined trade barrier (tariffs and QRs) on apparel imported from Hong Kong was more than twice as high when compared to apparel from USA, Canada and Japan which do not face quantitative restrictions in the EEC or EFTA. This study states that if Sweden removed such quota restrictions on apparel imported from LDCs, prices of imported apparel in Sweden would fall. If the entire reduction in import prices was passed on to the consumers, retail prices would fall by a maximum of 17 per cent. A free trade regime in Sweden, including abolition of the 13 per cent tariff on clothing, would result in an average saving of SEK 800 per annum per household. It would be as much SEK 1,200 per annum for salaried families with children (Hamilton, 1984). This study advocates unilateral abolition of quantitative restrictions by Sweden so as to reduce Swedish consumer prices and raise real incomes. Studies such as these have been ignored by the protectionists in the developed countries as is evident from the extension of MFA to its fourth term. However, Sweden has taken a decision to withdraw from MFA in 1991.

## Restriction Intensifier

MFA quotas are defined on a country of destination basis. The total imports allowed from an exporting country are then broken into product categories. In the EEC while some product categories are given an upper limit volume quota, exports in other product categories are subject to a basket extractor mechanism. Increased exports in non-restricted product categories in the past have led to annual ceilings. In the US, Canada, Sweden and Finland similar mechanisms operate. The breakdown of country quotas into fine product categories has the effect of enhancing or intensifying the restrictive effect of the QRs. (One result is that an exporting country is given quotas in categories where it has little or no comparative advantage.) Frequently, quotas remain underutilised as there is no provision for inter-country transfer or exchange among exporting countries under MFA (except for ASEAN-EC agreement).

To make things worse in the case of India, each category is further divided by Indian authorities into smaller categories (as for 'knitted' and 'woven' or 'woollen' and 'non-woollen') or operation of several systems of quota allocations to export firms. Annual quotas are divided into sub-periods. Over-categorisation coupled with intricacies of quota allocation systems works as a restriction intensifier. This intensifier can be reduced by replacing category-wise quotas with an agreement ceiling for all types of apparel, i.e., one category only, as imposed by the importing countries, a country quota upper limit can be defined in terms of number of pieces of apparel and/or its standard yardage equivalent (SYEs) such as in the case of US SYEs for Group II ceilings. Each consignment imported can be debited to the exporting country's aggregate upper limit. In such a system, firms in an exporting country can diversify their product mix in relation to their country specific comparative advantages while confining within the upper quota limit.

This restriction intensifier can also be eliminated by replacing countrywise export quotas with global import quotas expressed in quantity terms. A global import quota would be administered at the point of import as is in the case of Australia which is not an MFA signatory. It would allow entry to imports irrespective of country of origin till the global ceiling was exhausted. Such global quotas would enhance international competition and eliminate secured access to markets. However, there is fear in certain quarters that large suppliers may cover markets by control over distribution or by dumping, etc. Dominant suppliers holding quotas would have to vacate markets to other exporters who may have become more competitive. Inefficient suppliers would lose out markets to efficient suppliers. However, this is possible only when there exists a free market which at present is not the case. It is true that under such a system quota rents will be appropriated by the trade in the importing country. However, this system will ensure that exporting country market shares in the importing country are based on competitive advantages rather than historically secured market access. There can be two ways of implementing such a system. *First*, directly replacing the current system with a global quantitative quota for each importing country with due advance notice to trade and industry. Such a system will have the potential of disrupting secured market access enjoyed by the 'privileged firms' in exporting countries. *Second*, enforcing an annual cutback of 33 per cent in all export country current upper limits and transfer of released quantities to a global quota in the importing country. All suppliers then compete with each other for shares of released quantities plus a given volume growth. In three years all trade can come under global import quotas. Naturally, therefore, such quotas, would have to be expressed in quantity and not value terms.

These undesirable features of the present trading regime in textiles are sufficient to seek an early return to the GATT regime. Unfortunately, MFA-IV will now run till 1991 along with these features. The LDC negotiators have failed to steer an early return to GATT. The Indian team at Geneva must also share the burden of this failure as its position was in no way able to influence the outcome of MFA-IV. India as a leader of the nonaligned LDCs could not even ensure a date by which textile trade could return to the GATT regime. The Indian position with respect to MFA was that derogation from the normal rules of GATT inherent in the discriminatory regime of the MFA should be terminated (Rajya Sabha, unstarred question 1707, dated 3 December 1985). This position had been formulated after consultations with other developing exporting countries. India participated in the meeting of Developing Countries Exporters of Textiles and Clothing held in Beijing from 4–8 March 1986. This meeting called for an implementation of multilateral commitments by the developed countries including those undertaken at the ministerial meeting of GATT contracting parties held in 1982 which called for substantial liberalisation of restraints and phasing out of the MFA under an agreed time-frame. The Indian position had been that MFA had to be liberalised and phased out under an agreed time-frame. MFA-IV which India has now acceded to runs counter to this position. Apart from the fact that the Indian government owes an explanation not only to its own parliament but also to other interests in LDCs about the failure of the LDC negotiators, MFA-IV stands as a monument to the 'neo' protectionism.

MFA-IV is still more restrictive in its coverage as it now covers not only textiles and clothing of cotton, wool and man-made fibres but also vegetable fibres or blends thereof and blends containing silk. The rationale given is that such fibres are directly competitive products of cotton, wool or man-made fibres manufactured in the importing countries (see para 24 MFA-IV protocol). It states that all the member countries want an application of GATT rules to trade in textiles but falls short of mentioning any date for phasing out MFA. It also talks of liberalisation of QRs and increased market access to LDCs (paras 3 and 4). It also provides for liberal treatment to small suppliers, new entrants and least developed countries, especially cotton suppliers (para 13) and wool exporters (para 14). However, past experience has shown that such homilies give very little in terms of real market access. MFA-IV institutionalises bilateralism in the trade of textile and clothing as it provides for lower growth rates or even cutbacks under bilateral agreements (paras 9, 10 and 11). It introduces a new dimension to causes of market disruption—declining growth in per capita consumption of textiles and clothing. Such a declining growth is now a relevant factor to the recurrence or exacerbation of market disruption, even though factors listed in Annex A of MFA are the guiding principles on the whole. MFA-IV represents the continuation of the restrictive features of its first three extensions. By and large it has paved the ground for increasing bilateralism and moving further away from GATT rules.

The latest round of multilateral trade negotiations under GATT known as the Uruguay Round is now in a position of stalemate (as of April 1991). The US administration no longer dictates the outcome on all agenda items as a result of the emergence of a multipolar world where the European community, Japan and the group of non-aligned developing countries (G-77) have also become important negotiating blocks. Japan has reversed roles to become an importer of textiles. The textiles trade matrix now has three major importing regions—EC, North America and Nordics and three major developing country textile exporting blocks: (a) The major exporters represented by the East Asian Newly Industrialising Countries (NICs) of South Korea, Hong Kong and Taiwan which enjoy major market shares. (b) Middle level exporters who felt comfortable with secured market access in the early 1980s have begun to feel the pinch of quotas as their textile exports have slowly increased, even though they still remain marginal suppliers to the major textile importers. These include China, India, Pakistan, Indonesia, Brazil to name a few. The third block of developing country exporters much larger in number, are the sub-marginal suppliers who are not unhappy with the MFA and appear to be satisfied with secured market access. All these three blocks of developing exporting countries seek to revert textile trade to the GATT regime in their public postures. However, there appears to be a visible coincidence of interests among the sub-marginal suppliers and the East Asian NICs for the continuation of the MFA. This was perhaps one reason for the isolation of India and Brazil which were opposed to the fourth extension of MFA during the 1986 negotiations.

The effort to phase out MFA during the 1986 negotiations has been described as a 'puny push' led by a 'timid or terrified band of loosely organised textile/clothing exporter nations'. These efforts were no match for the massive lobbying by the US industry having an iron grip on key US Congressmen and negotiators as well as multilateral manoeuvering by US and EC negotiators. 'There were dark rumours that the phase out agenda may have been articulated, controlled, and scuttled by several member states who secretly viewed their interests as being better served by yet another extension of the quota regime' (Tuttle, 1987). This position is no different during the Uruguay Round as trade in textiles and clothing is one of the four major agenda items apart from subjects of agriculture, safeguards and intellectual property rights. The negotiation group on textiles and clothing reiterated the Punta del Este declaration to begin negotiations during 1989 'on modalities that could permit the eventual integration of this sector into GATT, on the basis of strengthened GATT rules and disciplines, thereby also contributing to the objective of further liberalisation of trade' (GATT Secretariat, 1988). However, no positive steps to dismantle MFA emerged. The only credible threat to MFA would be by the exporting countries to collectively apply trade sanctions if the MFA was continued. This, however, looks unlikely as East Asian NICs are apparently not interested in free trade in textiles because the current quotas give them a lion's share of the market that remains protected from the block of marginal suppliers who are gaining competitiveness. The sub-marginal suppliers are apprehensive of losing their secured market shares under a GATT regulated free trade regime. Hence, any major effort to revert textiles to the GATT regime can only be initiated by large countries which are marginal suppliers such as India, China, Indonesia and Brazil among others by forging a major political initiative in that direction.

# 2

# India's Apparel Exports: Importance, Direction and Composition

Textiles and clothing exports accounted for 6.5 per cent global merchandise exports during 1987. Global clothing exports of US $ 82 billion had surpassed global textile exports of US $ 80 billion for the first time in that year. While both textiles and clothing were subject to the MFA, value of clothing exports rose by 28.5 per cent, far exceeding textile export growth of 19.5 per cent in 1987. Between 1980 and 1986 world textile and clothing exports rose at an average rate of 3 per cent and 7.5 per cent respectively. Among the leading exporters were the four East Asian giants—South Korea, Hong Kong, China and Taiwan. During 1980–86 textile and clothing export growth rates of these four giants varied between 6.5 to 14.5 per cent in case of textiles and 9 to 11 per cent in case of clothing. In 1987 these four East Asian suppliers exported 33 per cent of world apparel exports. India ranked seventh with a share of 1.8 per cent. Turkey and Thailand which were way behind in 1980 have overtaken India in the recent years (see Table 3). Indian clothing exports rose from US $ 0.59 billion in 1980 to US $ 1.44 billion in 1987. India's textile exports, however, declined from US $ 1.14 billion to US $ 0.96 billion between 1980 and 1986. The rupee equivalents, however, showed growth merely due to the continuous devaluation of the Indian rupee.

In rupee terms Indian exports grew by 29 per cent in 1988–89 with textiles and apparel as the leading export earner. The country's exports no longer depend on a few items but are spread over a wide and diversified base. Table 4 shows that growth in textiles and apparel is being outpaced by higher growth in other products. The government of India has set an ambitious export target of Rs. 280 billion for 1989–90 representing a targeted growth of 38.2 per cent over the previous year. After textiles and apparel, the major exports are gems and jewellery, engineering products, agricultural products, leather products, chemical and allied products and minerals. All these product groups were targeted for higher export growth during 1989–90. The lower growth for textiles and apparel in part due to the protectionist barriers under the MFA.

Table 3

*Relative Shares of Global Apparel Exports from Leading Developing Countries, 1980–88*

|  | 1980 | 1985 | 1986 | 1987 | 1988 | |
|---|---|---|---|---|---|---|
|  | (%) | (%) | (%) | (%) | (%) | Rank |
| Hong Kong | 11.8 | 13.7 | 13.1 | 13.1 | 11.8 | (1) |
| South Korea | 7.1 | 9.0 | 8.6 | 9.2 | 8.7(2) | |
| Taiwan | 5.8 | 7.1 | 6.6 | 6.1 | 4.7 | (3) |
| China | 4.0 | 4.2 | 4.6 | 4.6 | 4.9 | (4) |
| Turkey | 0.3 | 2.5 | 2.0 | 2.7 | 2.4 | (5) |
| Thailand | 0.6 | 1.2 | 1.3 | 1.8 | 1.8 | (6) |
| India | 1.4 | 1.8 | 1.7 | 1.8 | 1.6 | (7) |
| **World apparel exports ($ bn)** | **41.8** | **49.2** | **63.8** | **81.9** | **80.9** | |

Source: GATT, "International Trade 87–88", Volume II

Table 4

*Indian Export Targets, 1989–90*

|  |  | Actuals 1988/89 (Rs. mn) | Target 1989/90 (Rs. mn) | Growth (%) |
|---|---|---|---|---|
| I | Textiles and Apparel | 45,860 | 55,000 | 20 |
| II | Gems and jewellery | 42,910 | 65,000 | 51.4 |
| III | Engineering goods | 22,580 | 30,000 | 39.5 |
| IV | Agricultural and allied products | 17,700 | 25,000 | 41.2 |
| V | Leather & its manufactures | 14,630 | 20,000 | 36.7 |
| VI | Chemicals and allied products | 13,380 | 30,000 | 116 |
| VII | Minerals and ores | 10,690 | 16,000 | 49.7 |
| **Total** | | **202,810** | **280,250** | **38.2** |

Source: FIEO Bulletin, August 1989

The importance of textile exports to India has relatively declined over the last three decades. Textile, made-ups and yarn exports occupied a place of pride during the 1950s and the 1960s. Over the 1970s and the 1980s apparel exports have overtaken that of other textiles.

Apparel exports accounted for a share of 7.28 per cent in India's total exports during 1984–85 as compared to 6.15 per cent over the previous year. On the other hand, all the other products of the textile complex (like fabrics, yarn and made-ups) put together accounted for only 5.17 per cent during 1984–85 as compared to 4.45 per cent in the previous year. However, exports of the textile complex have surged forward in 1988–89 raising their share from 12.5 per cent of India's total exports in 1984–85 to 20.9 per cent in 1988–89. The apparel sector maintained itself as the leading export sector in 1988–89. It was earlier believed that export of non-apparel textiles could not grow due to government restraints on industrial licensing policy which led to inefficiency of firms and a situation of domestic demand pressure.[1] However, a steady growth in exports of yarns, fabrics and made-ups between 1983 and 1989 appears to be linked to the structural changes in the weaving and spinning sectors.

Apparel exports were almost non-existent in the early 1970s, at a time when other textile products were a relatively important item of export. However, comparative advantage being allowed to play its role, apparel exports have been steadily growing over the last two decades. During 1970–71 apparel exports were a meagre Rs. 125 million but they rose to Rs. 2625.5 million during 1976–77 and Rs. 6,698 million in 1981–82. Data for calendar year 1985 show a figure of Rs. 10,676.5 million—an increase of almost eighty-five times over 1970–71. In 1986, 1988,1989 and 1990 they crossed the Rs. 13,000, Rs. 20,000, Rs. 30,000 and Rs. 40,000 million marks respectively. It will be observed that except for 1982, exports have been rising both in value and quantum terms (see Table 2). The marginal fall experienced in 1982, and the marginal increase of 1983 was mainly due to decrease in exports to the EEC. Exports to EEC have, however, accelerated from 1984 onwards. Trade watchers attribute the decline in exports to the EEC during 1982 and 1983 partly due to a 'not so hot' summer in Europe accompanied by a fashion swing during these years. Considering the fact that Indian apparel exports are cotton dominated, a

---

[1] See Jain, S.K. Export Performance and Export Marketing Strategies. Commonwealth Publishers, Delhi 1988.

cold summer in Europe adversely affects Indian exports. Another reason attributed is abrupt changes in fashion which may be beyond the reach of Indian materials and skills. The rising exports showed signs of levelling off in 1988 with only 3.2 per cent quantum increase in 1988. Growth in value terms, however, continues unabated. 1989 exports showed the highest ever value growth and over 25 per cent growth in quantity terms.

## DIRECTION OF APPAREL EXPORTS

Indian apparel was exported to 125 countries during 1985. Of the total exports of Rs. 10,676.5 million (255.9 million pieces) 97.4 per cent by value and 96.8 per cent by quantity were accounted for by only twenty-one countries. Of these countries, sixteen imposed quantitative restrictions, one country imposed a global tariff quota (Australia), two countries (Japan and Switzerland) used other NTBs (not a subject of study here) and two centrally planned economies—USSR, which imposed limits under bilateral trade plans, and Hungary, which administered imports. The remaining 104 countries accounted for only 2.6 per cent and 3.2 per cent of the total value and quantity respectively of Indian apparel exports in 1985. This direction of apparel exports has substantially remained the same over the 1980s.

The bulk of Indian exports were directed to the aforementioned two groups of markets over the period under study. The first group of countries of sixteen Western MFA signatories consists of the USA, the EEC (ten), Norway, Sweden, Finland, Austria and Canada. These quota countries accounted for 73.2 per cent by value (75.4 per cent by quantity) of India's total apparel exports during 1985. The other group of five countries accounted for only 24.2 per cent by value (21.4 per cent by quantum) of India's total exports in the same year. Table 5 shows that the direction of exports has more or less followed the same trend since 1980. The importance of the sixteen quota markets was maintained even in 1988.

The share of quota countries has fluctuated between 65.8 per cent and 81.6 per cent, of India's total apparel exports during the period under reference. Over the 1980s these quota countries have imported nearly three-fourths to four-fifths of Indian apparel exports both in quantity and value terms. The first group of sixteen quota countries constitutes India's major market for apparel today. The largest markets within these quota countries are the USA and the countries of the EEC—the major partners in the MFA. Any impact of QRs on the Indian apparel industry is in fact the impact on four-fifth of India's total apparel exports. This study, therefore, confines itself to an analysis of Indian exports to its quota markets.

Table 5

*Percentage Share of Exports*

| Years: | | 1980 | 1981 | 1982 | 1983 | 1984 | 1985 | 1988 |
|---|---|---|---|---|---|---|---|---|
| 16 Quota Countries | V | 78.4 | 72.3 | 65.8 | 75.9 | 75.3 | 73.2 | 79.6 |
| | Q | 81.6 | 67.8 | 68.0 | 75.0 | 76.4 | 75.4 | 78.3 |
| 5 Non-Quota Countries | V | na | 22.1 | 26.7 | 19.4 | 20.6 | 24.2 | 15.7 |
| | Q | na | 25.9 | 25.1 | 19.7 | 19.3 | 21.4 | 15.0 |

**Source :** Compound from AEPC Data.

## PRODUCT COMPOSITION OF APPAREL EXPORTS

The bulk of India's apparel exports to the sixteen quota countries is subject to QRs and a very small share consists of quota free items. Table 6 shows that except for Norway and Austria each of the quota markets restrains a bulk of Indian apparel exports. Norway and Austria account for an insignificant share (less than 1 per cent) in India's apparel exports and their non-imposition of severe quantitative restraints does not alter the total picture of QRs for India. The QRs imposed by the USA, countries of the EEC and Sweden are most comprehensive. They impose country/category upper limits on several sensitive categories. Categories not subject to upper limits are subject to Group II aggregate ceilings[2] in USA and the basket extractor mechanism in EEC. The result is that over 90 per cent of

[2] Indo-US bilateral agreement under MFA-III contained two groups, Group I consisting of textiles and Group II consisting of apparel. Within Group II there were product categories subject to ceilings as well as categories not subject to ceilings. However, there was an additional Group II ceiling covering all types of apparel. A category not subject to a ceiling would come under restraint once the Group II aggregate ceiling was reached. Under para 4 of the bilateral agreement that is valid from 1987 to 1991 (MFA-IV) their agreement structure has been modified. Group I now includes specific limits for specified categories while Group II includes other textiles and apparel items not subject to individual ceilings. They are, however, subject to the overall Group II ceiling.

the exports to the USA, EEC and Sweden consists of quota items and the levels for Finland and Canada are 75.1 per cent and 64.3 per cent respectively. QRs have generally become more restrictive during MFA-III particularly in Italy, UK, Ireland and Finland.

Norway which had initially opted out of MFA-III did not have a bilateral agreement with India during 1982–84. During 1981, 98.5 per cent of exports to Norway were subject to QRs. However, after it rejoined MFA, it reduced the number of items subject to QRs. In 1985, only 40.4 per cent of Indian items were subject to restraints. Absence of MFA type quotas in Norway during 1983–84 could have been a model representing the shape of things in the absence of MFA if Norway had not been such a small market. Indian exports to Norway during this period initially declined during 1982 and 1983, but staged a recovery in 1984 which continued into 1985.

Table 6

*Composition of Apparel Exports: Quantum Share of Quota Items (in per cent)*

|  | 1981 | 1982 | 1983 | 1984. | 1985 |
|---|---|---|---|---|---|
| U.S.A. | 79.4 | 84.9 | 97.8 | 96.0 | 92.7 |
| EEC | 92.3 | 96.4 | 99.3 | 99.7 | 99.7 |
| West Germany | 92.8 | 96.3 | 99.9 | 99.8 | 99.9 |
| France | 95.0 | 97.0 | 99.5 | 99.9 | 99.5 |
| Italy | 88.3 | 88.8 | 95.6 | 99.3 | 99.8 |
| Benelux | 96.3 | 97.7 | 99.8 | 100.0 | 99.9 |
| Denmark | 95.9 | 98.1 | 99.9 | 99.9 | 99.9 |
| U.K. | 90.0 | 98.3 | 99.6 | 99.6 | 99.4 |
| Ireland | 88.5 | 91.8 | 99.3 | 100.0 | 99.8 |
| Greece | 92.4 | 93.9 | 100.0 | 100.0 | 98.3 |
| Norway | 98.5 | OBA* | OBA | OBA | 40.4 |
| Sweden | 99.7 | 99.6 | 97.2 | 99.4 | 99.3 |
| Finland | 33.8 | 21.4 | 83.3 | 83.7 | 75.1 |
| Austria | 37.8 | 43.9 | 15.7 | 19.5 | 22.0 |
| Canada | 87.8 | 92.4 | 89.8 | 67.0 | 64.3 |

Source: Computed from AEPC Data
*Outside Bilateral Agreement

Canada has been one country where the severity of restrictions has been declining in terms of the share of Indian exports subject to restraints during MFA-III. The restrained items share of 92.4 per cent in 1982 has come down to 64.3 per cent in 1985.

The share of quota items has been on the higher side even after 1985 and import restrictions have by and large intensified even under MFA-IV. Indian exports to major markets have, however, continued to rise to quota as well as non-quota markets. Table 7 shows the detailed break-up of rising apparel exports to India's major markets over the 1980s.

## PRIMARY PRODUCT SPECIALISATION

The global apparel industry produces a very broad range of products. However, in each country the specialisation at the firm level tends to take the shape of extremely narrow product specialisation in a handful of products. An illustrative example is that of the US apparel industry. One study computed primary product specialisation (PPS) ratios[3] (Arpan, De La Torre and Toyne, 1982) of US apparel firms along several apparel industry segments. These ratios were between 83 and 99 per cent in the case of eleven US apparel industry segments. Product concentration ratios were also found to be high in most segments of the US apparel industry. Such high PPS ratios signify heavy dependence on one product at the firm level. Such high product concentration in US firms made them vulnerable to import competition as it is also an indication of inability to substitute in production. In the words of the above-mentioned study: 'the production techniques, equipment and skills necessary for the manufacture of women's blouses are not readily transferable to the manufacture of women's suits and jackets. Vulnerability to imports was further aggravated by the fact that most apparel firms had single product operations. Such establishments were unable to respond to surges in imports of a particular apparel product by changing product lines and thus were severely hampered in their ability to modify product strategies' (Arpan, De La Torre and Toyne, 1982).

The Indian apparel industry is also in a similar situation in so far as its primary product specialisation tends to be very high. Detailed data for various industry segments are non-existent. There are no data on the number of establishments, employment, product specialisation, sales, etc., available even with the government of India (see

---

[3] Primary product specialisation ratio describes the proportion of product shipments (both primary and secondary) of the industry segment represented by primary products.

Table 7
Direction of Apparel Exports (1980–1988)

| | | 1980 | 1981 | 1982 | 1983 | 1984 | 1985 | 1986 | 1987 | 1988 |
|---|---|---|---|---|---|---|---|---|---|---|
| Global | V | 4334.9 | 6500.3 | 6335.7 | 6401.3 | 8500.8 | 10676.5 | 13231.2 | 18574.3 | 21486.4 |
| | Q | (141.3) | (199.0) | (187.0) | (193.4) | (230.6) | (255.9) | (300.8) | (370.1) | (396.7) |
| All Quota countries | V | 3554.9 | 4697.4 | 4278.0 | 4856.1 | 6401.1 | 7811.5 | 10350.9 | 15285.6 | 17230.8 |
| | Q | (115.3) | (134.9) | (127.2) | (145.1) | (176.2) | (192.9) | (236.1) | (299.7) | (313.0) |
| USA | V | 972.5 | 1375.6 | 1384.8 | 2258.8 | 2914.6 | 3464.1 | 4403.8 | 6048.4 | 6639.3 |
| | Q | (37.2) | (48.4) | (48.8) | (70.1) | (78.5) | (74.0) | (83.8) | (102.0) | (102.3) |
| EEC | V | 2353.4 | 2869.1 | 2491.3 | 2162.0 | 2809.4 | 3425.7 | 5032.6 | 8120.9 | 9421.7 |
| | Q | (70.2) | (73.9) | (67.1) | (63.1) | (80.0) | (97.4) | (133.5) | (175.4) | (187.8) |
| Norway | V | 36.2 | 44.8 | 35.0 | 32.4 | 49.9 | 62.4 | 65.99 | 89.28 | 79.72 |
| | Q | (1.1) | (1.2) | (1.0) | (0.9) | (1.2) | (1.5) | (1.2) | (1.6) | (1.3) |
| Sweden | V | 108.1 | 142.3 | 128.8 | 131.9 | 160.3 | 182.3 | 224.3 | 297.7 | 248.2 |
| | Q | (3.9) | (4.1) | (3.5) | (3.4) | (4.3) | (4.3) | (4.6) | (5.6) | (4.5) |
| Finland | V | 9.3 | 31.1 | 39.6 | 25.6 | 30.2 | 41.5 | 71.5 | 89.1 | 74.8 |
| | Q | (0.3) | (0.8) | (1.8) | (1.2) | (1.0) | (1.2) | (1.8) | (2.4) | (1.9) |
| Austria | V | 20.5 | 61.1 | 71.2 | 58.1 | 51.7 | 49.0 | 73.4 | 130.9 | 168.1 |
| | Q | (0.6) | (1.4) | (1.6) | (1.6) | (1.2) | (1.1) | (1.7) | (3.4) | (3.8) |
| Canada | V | 54.4 | 173.4 | 162.3 | 214.6 | 435.1 | 586.6 | 479.4 | 509.2 | 599.0 |
| | Q | (1.9) | (5.2) | (4.4) | (5.7) | (11.0) | (13.3) | (9.4) | (9.4) | (11.4) |
| All Non-quota countries | V | 780.0 | 1799.7 | 2057.7 | 1545.2 | 2099.7 | 2865.0 | 2880.3 | 3288.7 | 4255.6 |
| | Q | (26.0) | (64.1) | (59.8) | (48.3) | (54.4) | (63.0) | (64.7) | (70.4) | (83.7) |

(Table 7 Contd.)

| | | 1980 | 1981 | 1982 | 1983 | 1984 | 1985 | 1986 | 1987 | 1988 |
|---|---|---|---|---|---|---|---|---|---|---|
| Australia | V | NA | 98.9 | 130.1 | 104.5 | 208.6 | 175.3 | 169.0 | 225.4 | 304.6 |
| | Q | NA | (2.9) | (3.0) | (2.3) | (3.1) | (3.0) | (3.0) | (3.6) | (4.5) |
| Japan | V | NA | 156.9 | 183.3 | 143.2 | 236.5 | 404.5 | 333.0 | 376.3 | 503.7 |
| | Q | NA | (5.0) | (5.3) | (4.1) | (6.2) | (9.6) | (8.2) | (7.9) | (8.8) |
| Switzerland | V | NA | 213.2 | 179.0 | 203.3 | 176.9 | 196.0 | 320.3 | 439.6 | 497.1 |
| | Q | NA | (16.6) | (10.1) | (14.5) | (10.4) | (6.6) | (10.3) | (13.7) | (12.9) |
| USSR | V | NA | 952.5 | 1171.4 | 732.7 | 1057.0 | 1725.9 | 1568.4 | 1663.8 | 2040 |
| | Q | NA | (25.6) | (25.9) | (14.2) | (22.2) | (32.9) | (29.3) | (28.2) | (31.8) |
| Hungary | V | NA | 18.2 | 30.9 | 57.5 | 70.2 | 80.7 | 77.0 | 44.9 | 40.1 |
| | Q | NA | (1.4) | (2.7) | (3.1) | (2.5) | (2.7) | (2.1) | (1.0) | (1.5) |

Source: AEPC Annual Data 1980 to 1988

Notes : Value(V) : In million Rs.
Quantity(Q) : In million pcs.

Lok Sabha unstarred question No. 4689 dated 24 August 1984). It is impossible to work out PPS or concentration ratios for the Indian apparel industry. The only reliable data available on this industry pertain to its export sector. An analysis of the data for the period under reference reveals that during 1985, 64.9 per cent of Indian exports to sixteen quota countries consisted of four primary products, namely: blouses and shirts; ladies dresses; skirts; and trousers.

Table 8 shows the quantum and the value shares of these four products taken as a group in the entire product range of all segments of the Indian garment industry.

### Table 8

*Primary Products Specialisation in India's Apparel
Exports (percentage)*

| Destinations | | 1980 | 1981 | 1982 | 1983 | 1984 | 1985 | 1986 | 1987 | 1988 |
|---|---|---|---|---|---|---|---|---|---|---|
| 16 Quota | Q | 79.4 | 71.0 | 69.1 | 74.1 | 65.8 | 64.9 | 64.1 | 64.7 | 62.8 |
| Countries | V | 78.2 | 71.3 | 75.6 | 73.6 | 66.6 | 70.0 | 69.8 | 67.4 | 66.6 |
| USA + EEC*(10) | Q | 79.3 | 70.7 | 72.6 | 74.3 | 66.3 | 65.6* | 63.0 | 63.1 | 61.3 |
| | V | 77.4 | 71.1 | 76.4 | 73.6 | 67.3 | 70.6 | 69.0 | 66.0 | 65.3 |
| 5 other Quota | Q | 80.4 | 74.4 | 64.0 | 72.2 | 61.7 | 59.9 | 77.3 | 85.4 | 82.2 |
| Countries | V | 89.6 | 73.4 | 69.0 | 73.4 | 60.7 | 64.9 | 77.9 | 86.0 | 84.5 |

**Source:** Computed From AEPC Data.
*1986, 1987, 1988 data are for EEC (12).

It will be observed that the PPS ratio[4] has slowly declined over the last six years. The PPS ratio in this case represents the share of primary products in total exports to the named markets. This ratio is still quite high despite the slow decline over the period under reference. A high PPS ratio in the case of Indian apparel exports signifies a narrow range of product specialisation for the country as a whole. Even without firm level data, it can be stated that such specialisation at the firm level would turn out to be much narrower in the context of a large number of small export firms in India.

The PPS ratios have been constructed on the basis of export statistics maintained by AEPC. Such disaggregated statistics are available only for these sixteen quota countries and not for other countries. However, it would not be off the mark to draw an inference that these PPS ratios are common to the whole export sector of the

---

[4] Defined as the share of four primary apparel products in India's total exports of apparel to stated destinations.

industry primarily because the bulk of Indian exports are directed to developed countries having similar clothing habits.

If one examines the changes in the composition of apparel exports country by country, the trend is unmistakable. These four primary products dominate each and every market except that of Italy. The share of these four apparel items in exports to each of the countries has been maintained. There was a small decline in 1983 and 1984 in Benelux and Denmark which was restored in 1985 along with an increase in the share of secondary items—particulary non-restricted and quota free items during this period. The dominance of these four primary items is even visible in small quota markets like Greece, Ireland and Norway.

The only variation in this trend of dominance of primary products in apparel exports is the case of the Italian market. The quantum share of *primary product* exports to Italy has declined by 35.1 per cent from 1980 to 1985. However the decline in terms of value is only 9.5 per cent. The decline in quantum share is due to falling shares of all primary product exports except gents shirts. This fall has been offset by an increase in share of non-restricted items which has risen to 63.35 per cent in 1985. These items also include quota categories which are not subject to upper limits. Apparently since the value contribution of the primary products has declined by only 9.5 per cent, the following inference can be drawn on the basis of country-wise data. In 1985 there was an increase in exports to Italy of 152 per cent in quantum and 49 per cent in value. This increase was mainly due to a sharp rise in exports of secondary products (non-restricted) of 430 per cent by quantum and 142 per cent by value. The increase was mainly due to low price secondary products, including cotton knitwear. While the 1985 average export price of primary products was Rs. 36.83, the average price of secondary products was only Rs. 11.01 in the same year. To our mind such a large increase in low price secondary product exports to Italy has a linkage with the changes taking place in the Italian apparel industry itself.

According to a study conducted by the UNCTAD (UNCTAD, 1984) Italy has been able to expand its apparel output and minimise employment losses largely due to its small-scale enterprises based on 'productive decentralisation' using 'black labour' (i.e., not paying taxes and not subject to social security). According to this study 'The structure of production appears more important in explaining the success of the industry than the advantages of "black labour". It is probably in activities where the minimum viable scale is small, and which virtually is carried out in the home, that "black" labour becomes as important as the structure of production in explaining competitiveness'. Black labour in this context refers to labour engaged in violation of minimum wages and other municipal laws. The organisation of production in Italy is done on a subcontracting basis wherein small, independent firms enjoying financial and organisational economies specialise in certain manufacturing functions. This study refers to the period around the beginning of MFA-III and subsequent changes in Italian industry are not known. It is, however, probable that Italian costs of production may be on the rise inducing demand for lower cost imports in new product segments which fall outside India's primary product specialisation. Italian apparel exports have captured large shares of the EEC market as the trade diversion impact of MFA quotas. This may have resulted in increasing production costs in Italy so as to induce an import demand for low price non-restricted imports of the type India exported to Italy in 1985 at average price of Rs. 11 a piece—less than one US $ FOB.

Despite the unique case of the Italian market it is true that composition of India's apparel exports is dominated by four primary products. It is also true that each of these four primary products is subject to QRs with ceilings at the category level in each of the quota markets.

# 3

# Working of the Quota Regime

Macroeconomists generally believe that quotas do not become binding till 100 per cent quotas are utilised. Such a generalisation cannot be made unless one examines the working of a quota distribution regime. It is possible for quotas to become binding even at levels below 100 per cent depending on how they are administered. The quota regime in India provides a case study to show how quotas can become binding at utilisation levels below 100 per cent. Let us examine how such a situation emerges.

The quantitative levels agreed under the bilaterals negotiated within the framework of MFA are set down for each category for each country of destination. Annual levels set apart for each country/category in terms of volume of apparel signify the maximum volume the country is allowed to ship within each quota year (usually on a twelve month basis). However, since there are over 8,000 firms in the apparel industry differing with respect to their market and product specialisations, the distribution of an annual quota amongst mutually competing firms is not a simple matter. The government of India formulates a policy for distribution of quota among firms in the industry on a year to year basis. The implementation of this policy is delegated to the Apparel Export Promotion Council (AEPC) which is an autonomous body managed by the elected representatives of registered apparel exporters.

The impact of MFA-I was hardly felt by the Indian apparel trade and industry. Until 1977–78, the level of quota utilisations was quite low and free quotas were available. It was during the period of

MFA-II and MFA-III that quota utilisation levels started rising and restricting the Indian exports. Annual quotas are disaggregated to give an upper limit for each restrained category. During MFA-II and MFA-III it has been seen that product categories having a higher demand in a particular year or season (sub-period) got exhausted and there were no takers for other categories. 'Swing' provisions come in only when annual levels have been exhausted. During sub-period exhaustions swings do not help to increase the quota availability. This results in the unutilised quotas at end of the quota period. The familiar protectionist argument that quotas did not hurt the exporter as quotas had not been fulfilled may not stand scrutiny as the impact of these quotas cannot be observed simply by examining year-end quota utilisations. To understand the real impact it would be necessary to examine the manner in which country/category based quotas are actually administered at the point of export. All QR-bilaterals leave the quota administration to the exporting country. It would, therefore, be appropriate to examine the effect of the policy relating to the distribution of annual levels among different firms in the trade and industry.

The Indian quota distribution policy divides the firms into different categories: (a) There are sets of rules applicable to each category of firms which must be followed by a firm to seek a quota allocation against a confirmed export order backed by an irrevocable letter of credit. (b) Sets of floor prices are laid down below which no firm is allowed to export. Subject to the floor prices a firm can seek quota allocations under the two basic types of quota: 'open' and 'closed' The 'closed' quota is available only to firms having a past performance of export. This arrangement reserves a certain quota for established exporters in a given product and country of destination. The past performance is determined with reference to a relevant base period. Manufacturer-exporters in the organised sector listed with the government and having well established production facilities also have access to this section being guaranteed a small quota volume. This section is closed to new firms or firms that do not have a past performance of exports. The 'open' section is available to firms without any past performance. Such open quota allocations are made on a 'first come first serve' (FCFS) basis. The working of the overall policy reveals the following five salient features:

1. Floor Prices

2. Closed Allocations
3. Open Allocations and Cut Off Prices
4. Closed vs Open Allocations
5. Over-Categorisation

## Floor Prices

The AEPC works out minimum export prices for each category of garments exported to a given destination on the basis of manufacturing costs and export prices. These minimum prices are known as floor prices and tend to represent minimum labour and material costs based on domestic prices. Export below floor prices is not allowed due to two reasons. First to discourage under-invoicing of exports that can result in a drain on foreign exchange from national export earnings. Secondly, to discourage unhealthy price undercutting among Indian exporters for gaining export orders. Floor prices were initially introduced to avoid massive undercutting of prices by Indian firms as apparel exports began to grow during MFA-I and a large number of new firms entered the apparel export trade. New entrants had little or no experience in the trade and cut prices to attract importers. Having accepted orders at low prices, they frequently shipped out inferior quality merchandise. This adversely affected the image of Indian apparel in export markets. It was only then that floor prices were introduced. At that time QRs on Indian apparel were not binding in almost all destinations.

Indian authorities justify use of floor prices on grounds that Indian firms must export higher unit value products. Since market disruption is said to be caused due to low cost imports, LDC firms must·export more and more higher price products to come out of the 'low cost syndrome'. Using this argument Indian authorities are raising floor prices from year to year. A rough method used to fix floor prices in the current year is the 'mean' price of all exports in a given country/category during the past year. The floor price is generally on the lower side of this mean price.

Floor prices generally represent the threshold of prices below which exports would become uneconomical for all but the most efficient firms. They are worked out keeping in view the average labour costs, consumption of fabric in different apparel sizes, fabric prices in the home market as well as prices prevailing in export markets. They are determined separately for adult or children apparel as well as for knitted or woven fabric segments.

One view is that floor prices work against less efficient firms and enable the more efficient firms to get the export orders. This would ensure that the difference between domestic production costs and the given price in the importing country is the largest. This difference includes the quota rents. This was, however, not the reason for initial fixation of floor prices.

## 'Closed' Allocations

The annual quota level being a scarce commodity, a larger export volume than the quota available in a sub-period is sought by new and established firms. The allocation of quotas is determined by a policy which has evolved under the influence of established firms in the industry and has resulted in a bias against new firms entering the industry. The AEPC, whose views influence the government's policy formulations, is dominated by old and established exporters. This class of firms has steadily been increasing the shares of quota allocation in their own favour over the years. In 1986, 75 per cent of the annual level in a country/category was allocated on the basis of past performance to four types of firms in the class of old and established exporters:

### ■ Past Performance Quota ■

A firm having exported in past two-and-a-half years provided that it had an export performance in a country/category during any two of the three years in the base period. Sixty-five per cent of the annual level in a country/category is allocated to firms on the basis of such past performance. Such quota allocation is known as past performance (PP) quota. During 1984, 1,235 firms[1] were allocated such PP quotas. Their number during 1986 increased to about 1,500 firms. The allocations are made on a pro rata basis to applicants in each country/category. Since number of applicants per year is on the rise, a firm normally gets less than the volume exported in a given country/category during its previous year. While annual volume quotas and share for PP quotas have been growing, the growth in the number

[1] See Lok Sabha unstarred question No. 2031 dated 3 August 1984. Ministry of Commerce, Government of India.

of applicants in the scarce country/categories has outstripped growth in quotas available for PP quotas.

PP quotas are freely transferable after they have been allotted to the eligible firms. During MFA-III it was observed that such PP quotas began to be sold and bought in the market.

■ *Manufacturers Quota* ■

Seven per cent of the annual level in 1986 and 1987 was allocated to an estimated 300 manufacturers. These manufacturers represent the organised sector of the apparel industry. Eligible manufacturers have to conform to labour and factory laws to obtain manufacturers quota (MQ). Such exporters are allocated quantities in relation to their past performance as well as their manufacturing capacity.[2] Considering the fact that 8,260 firms were registered with AEPC in 1986 only 3.6 per cent of them belong to the organised manufacturing sector. A bulk of the manufacturing was emanating from the 'decentralised' sector which was not eligible for MQ allocations.

■ *Public Sector Quota* ■

Central and state government undertakings were allocated 3 per cent of annual quota levels. During 1985, nineteen such public sector corporations were allocated this quota (see Lok Sabha unstarred question no. 2823 dated 6 December 1985). The share of such allocations was reduced to 2 per cent in 1987. Prior to 1986 public sector companies took advantage of quota rents and allowed private sector exporters to use this quota for a price. However, since 1987 such applicants must have their own manufacturing facilities before they can get such quota allocations.

■ *Non-Quota Exporters* ■

For the first time in 1987 quota allocations are being used as an instrument for encouraging exports to non-quota destinations. One per cent of the annual level has been allocated for firms having a specified level of exports to non-quota destinations outside the eastern block.

[2] See Lok Sabha unstarred question No. 4599 dated 24 August 1984; also see Export Trade Control Public Notice No. 20-ETC(PN)/86 published in Part I, Section I, of the Gazette of India Extraordinary dated 6 October 1986.

## Open Allocations and Cut-Off Prices

Only 25 per cent of the annual level in a country/category remains after distributing 75 per cent under closed allocations. Allocations are made on a FCFS basis. New entrants in the industry, new entrants in a market or country/category can queue up for allocations on the basis of firm contracts backed by valid, operative and irrevocable letters of credit. This 25 per cent share is divided among three four-monthly sub-periods viz. January to April distributing 15 per cent; May to August with 7 per cent, and September to December with 3 per cent. Firms having quotas under closed allocations are also allowed to queue up for FCFS quota after they have used 50 per cent of their quotas or after surrendering their PPQ/MQ quotas in a country/category.

Such quotas must be used for shipment within sixty days of allotment. They are not transferable and do not enter the market for sale and purchase of quotas on transfer basis. This section is only 'half' open as new firms entering the industry are shut out for two-and-a-half years before they can be eligible for FCFS quotas. During 1986 firms registered after 1 January 1984 were shut out of this allocation. During 1987 firms registered after 1 July 1984 were shut out. Moreover, one firm cannot seek more than a few thousand pieces quota in a single application on any day.

The quota year was divided into three four-monthly periods for purpose of allocations from the open segment. The open portions of the quota share were further distributed in the ratio of 15:7:3 with the first period (January to April) getting the largest share. For certain items (knitwear), the quota year was divided into two sub-periods with the first period getting 85 per cent and the second period getting the balance.

Ostensibly this division of the quota year was done in view of spreading out exports throughout the year. However, such requirements did not apply to the quota allocations in the closed system.

There is a perpetual squeeze in open allocations. For many categories to destinations like USA and Sweden FCFS allocations exhaust on the first day of a quota sub-period triggering the quota premium market.

■ *Cut-Off Prices* ■

Since fashion and consumer preference in developed markets keep changing each year, there is no certainty that an export firm will get export orders from the same country/category. If it gets orders in another country/category, or if its PP quota is inadequate for a given export order, it must queue up for the FCFS system. A firm having no past performance can also queue up for an open allocation.

All applications for FCFS allotment are given quotas depending on the availability in this section. If on a given day the demand for quota allocation exceeds the availability, allotments are made on the basis of a cut-off price. The export prices of each application are arranged in the descending order. The list is divided on the basis of a price which 'cuts' the list in two parts and such that quantities demanded by applications above this price are equal to the quota available. Applications below the cut-off price are rejected. Firms obtaining orders after the exhaustion of this open section seek transfer of PP quotas on payment to PP quota holders by way of quota premia. A cut-off price in a country/category usually signals the activation of quota premia on PPQ transfers. As long as the cut-off price is not determined, quotas are available for the asking and no quota premium operates in the market. If some quantities are released due to surrender of unutilised PPQs, they may be placed on FCFS. The moment the quota in FCFS becomes available, the quota premium on transfer of PPQ almost disappears. It reappears again on the day the cut-off price is determined. In many cases export orders may have to be refused as export prices may not justify the quota premium. Such cut-off prices are not applicable to PPQ allotments.

## Open vs. Closed Section

Old and established exporters of apparel have steadily been able to expropriate larger shares of annual quota levels for closed allocations. This has been possible because the quota distribution policy has been promulgated by the government under increasing influence of old and established exporters in the AEPC. Table 9 shows the increasing share of the closed section in annual levels over the past six years.

The share in the open section has reduced from 55 to 25 per cent. This leaves a very small share of quotas for free allocation. Cut-off prices are declared within a few days of the opening of the quota periods. The quota premium market for PPQ transfers begins almost immediately. Firms holding PP quotas can utilise them up to

Table 9

*Quota Allocation Shares in Annual Levels*

|  | 1981 | 1982 | 1983 | 1984 | 1985 | 1986 | 1987 |
|---|---|---|---|---|---|---|---|
| *Open Section* | | | | | | | |
| FCFS | 55 | 45 | 35 | 35 | 30 | 25 | 25 |
| *Closed Section* | | | | | | | |
| PPQ | 40 | 45 | 50 | 50 | 55 | 65 | 65 |
| MQ | Bonus | Bonus | 10 | 10 | 10 | 7 | 7 |
| Public Sector | 5 | 5 | 5 | 5 | 5 | 3 | 2 |
| Non-Quota | - | - | - | - | - | - | 1 |

Source: Annual Quota Policies, AEPC.

30 September of the quota year. However, they should ship 50 per cent of the quantity by April. Delay in shipment involves forfeiture of earnest money deposits unless it is surrendered. Depending upon the demand for quotas, firms invariably delay surrendering quotas hoping to profit by quota premium on transfer. Availability of quotas on the open section, market expectations and sentiments play a large role in determining the surrender of PPQ by allottee export firms. There have been cases where firms sit on PPQ for nine months of the quota year. The surrender comes late by which time quota markets may have already triggered a premium. Availability of FCFS quota during the last period (October to December) due to such surrenders may not be helpful as there may be no demand for quotas at that time. This is particularly true because over 80 per cent of Indian apparel exports are made of cotton which have almost no market in the winter period. PPQ surrenders may show unutilised quantities at the year end, yet open section quotas are not available during the year.

Such PP based quota allocation is also reflected by another device that has evolved over the years. Till 1982 PP quota holders were not eligible for quota allocation under the open segment. However, since 1983 quota holders were allowed to seek quota allocations in the open segment after utilisation of half their PPQ allocations. Before as well as after 1983 quota holders sought larger and larger shares from the open segment. They floated new companies or firms for the major purpose of getting quota allocation from the open segment. All along (till 1984) a new firm registered with AEPC up to six months before the beginning of the quota year could seek quota allocations from the open segment. Large number of PP quota holders floated shadow firms/companies, got them registered with AEPC and sought allocations from the open segments. Conscious to this development, the government extended the requirement of six months prior registration to one year with effect from quota year 1985. This resulted in PP quota holders seeking take-overs of registered firms who were eligible for 'open' segment allocation. Take-overs of registered firms was for a price consideration, price reflecting the magnitude of quota rents involved. In 1986 this prior registration period was extended to two years. In order to restrain the PP quota holders from taking over eligible companies for cornering quotas, the 1986 policy[3] has excluded such associated concerns from seeking allocations from the 'open' segment.

The number of export firms registered with AEPC has shown a phenomenal rise between 1978 and 1986. This increase has been partly attributed to the registration of shadow/associated concerns for the purpose of 'quota cornering activity'. In fact the AEPC has been dominated by established exporters who have in their common interest taken up positions for increasing shares in the 'closed' system year after year. This is referred to as the 'quota cornering effect' and represents the individual firm's tendency to seek as large a share of quota entitlements as is possible without any regard for new firms entering the industry.

The data examined herein go on to prove the Hypothesis 3 'Quotas induce quota cornering activity among firms in the exporting country'.

## Over Categorisation

Quotas under the aegis of MFA are broken down categorywise for each exporting country and upper limits specified for each category. For example, USA has 104 categories based on the tariff schedule of USA. There are thirty-nine categories for cotton, twenty-four for wool and forty-one for man-made fibres. The groups under QRs differ from bilateral agreement to agreement (UNCTAD, 1984). Each group includes a large number of categories and is defined according to the type of the final products and their fibre content. India exports more than fifty-eight categories of apparel to USA of which QRs apply to about a dozen and there is an overall Group II ceiling on all apparel. Similarly EEC has categories based both on

[3] See para 2B (VIII) of Garment Export Entitlement Policy, 1986, AEPC.

NIMEXE codes and special MFA categories. Currently 114 categories are covered by the Indo–EEC textile agreement of which about forty belong to apparels. About a dozen of these are subject to QRs while non-restricted exports in other categories are subject to the basket extractor mechanism. There are two problems here. First, there are a large number of narrowly defined categories. Second, these narrow categories are subject to national quotas within the EEC. This results in the problem of over-categorisation.

Whenever upper limits are specified in respect of India, the Indian quota administration policy further adds to the over-categorisation by splitting the importing country's category into the sub-categories like knitted (K) handloom (H) mill-made (M). Another way in which over-categorisation has taken place at the export end is through dual price levels. During 1980 two price levels were specified—floor price (FP) and high price (HP) and the quantitative limit of the category divided among the two. While one sub-category exhausted, the other remained available in the open section resulting in binding restrictions at the firm level. Another type of categorisation is based on nature of fibre. For example, the Indian quota policy (1985 to 1987) reserves portions of annual levels for woollen apparel in several country/categories to similar effect. This is also a self-imposed division.

This splits the upper limit of the category into three parts depending on the pulls and pressures from trade and industry. The importing country does not make such distinctions. The result is that the mill-made section of the category may be exhausted while knitted and handloom remain unutilised. Firms may be unable to export mill-made type for non-availability of quota and the restriction becomes binding on the firm even when the category has not exhausted. This has happened on several occasions in the past.

The point that is being made here is that whenever an exporting country sets up limits within limits in a category, it intensifies the restrictions imposed by the importing country. Whenever such sub-limits are imposed they become binding on one section of the industry or the other. This is so because a firm has a limited product and market specialisation. Once a sub-limit exhausts, the firm is forced out of the market, contracts may have to be cancelled or quotas may have to be purchased from the market for a consideration. Hence such over-categorisation enhances the restriction effect of quotas. A scarce quota is a valuable asset and when not used it represents a want of resources. From the policy angle the exporting country must not impose sub-limits within upper limits and must allow all firms in the industry to compete for each unit of quota in the open section. This is something India can do on its own and without reference to the MFA or bilateral agreements. The evidence examined herein is sufficient to prove the hypothesis 'Over-categorisation acts as a restriction intensifier to enhance the trade restrictive effect of quotas.'

# 4

# Quota Utilisations and Comparative Advantage

It will be worthwhile to examine the aggregate quota utilisations over the period of MFA-II and MFA-III. This analysis is confined to six calendar years from 1980 to 1985. While four years 1982 to 1985 cover the MFA-III, data for 1980 and 1981 are used as a back-drop to the last two years of MFA-II.

The aggregate base level for an exporting country is expressed in terms of number of pieces of different types of apparel in a quota year. This base level is broken down into number of pieces for each category of apparel to give the category base level. The actual volume of exports at the end of a quota year expressed as a percentage of the aggregate base level gives the *aggregate quota utilisation*. Similarly the actual volume of exports in a category at the end of a quota year expressed as a percentage of the category base level gives the *category quota utilisation*. Table 10 shows that aggregate quota utilisations have been well below 100 per cent in each of the six years for all restrained markets except USA (during three years, 1983, 1984 and 1985). For the EEC, aggregate utilisations have never crossed 75 per cent, leading to the familiar protectionist argument that quotas do not hurt India as they are grossly underutilised. Data in Table 2 show that among the fourteen markets imposing QRs on exports of Indian apparel, there was not a single market where aggregate quota utilisations reached the ceilings during 1980 and 1982. There was only one market where utilisations crossed 100

## Table 10
### Market-wise Aggregate Quota Utilisations (percentage)

| Markets | 1980 | 1981 | 1982 | 1983 | 1984 | 1985 | 1986 | 1987 | 1988 |
|---|---|---|---|---|---|---|---|---|---|
| USA Gr.II | 78.1 | 75.5 | 69.7 | 109.8 | 102.1 | 100.2 | 109.75 | 119.24 | 102.41 |
| W. Germany | 82.8 | 78.6 | 73.2 | 53.0 | 54.0 | 74.8 | 102.13 | 110.59 | 108.18 |
| France | 94.9 | 88.5 | 72.0 | 57.7 | 59.9 | 70.6 | 92.76 | 106.51 | 109.80 |
| Italy | 79.9 | 63.1 | 44.9 | 51.2 | 40.0 | 51.4 | 88.35 | 106.10 | 70.25 |
| Benelux | 68.3 | 62.4 | 57.1 | 42.9 | 55.3 | 66.3 | 85.96 | 105.44 | 99.08 |
| Denmark | 87.4 | 86.6 | 83.8 | 76.4 | 77.9 | 89.1 | 108.07 | 98.57 | 85.01 |
| UK | 52.2 | 55.0 | 64.5 | 56.6 | 75.5 | 68.3 | 74.77 | 108.17 | 97.95 |
| Ireland | 40.0 | 64.9 | 56.5 | 51.8 | 58.1 | 68.0 | 73.47 | 106.20 | 88.11 |
| Greece | OBA | 66.7 | 41.4 | 37.2 | 63.2 | 76.3 | 61.77 | 46.48 | 19.63 |
| Spain | – | – | – | – | – | – | – | 61.68 | 101.82 |
| Portugal | – | – | – | – | – | – | – | 39.94 | 26.80 |
| EEC | 70.5 | 61.4 | 65.3 | 53.9 | 61.2 | 69.1 | 88.79 | 106.79 | 96.98 |
| Sweden | 99.8 | 105.1 | 87.7 | 74.8 | 101.8 | 100.9 | 105.66 | 114.65 | 88.85 |
| Finland | 72.0 | 53.2 | 76.7 | 63.6 | 54.4 | 56.4 | 78.48 | 77.81 | 54.62 |
| Austria | 70.3 | 55.2 | 67.6 | 95.1 | 89.3 | 88.6 | 99.65 | 108.40 | 104.06 |
| Canada | 68.6 | 75.3 | 63.3 | 73.6 | 98.9 | 108.0 | 78.71 | 91.34 | 100.87 |
| Norway | 27.8 | 34.5 | OBA | OBA | OBA | 96.1 | 92.29 | 101.03 | 76.34 |
| All | – | – | – | 73.2 | 76.4 | 79.8 | | | |

Sources : 1) LS US Q No.3839 dt. 19.4.85.
2) LS US Q No. 812 dt. 27.7.84.
3) Handbook of Export Statistics for Garments and Knitwear (1980–82), AEPC, New Delhi and AEPC unpublished statistical tables for 1983 to 1988.
4) Data for USA (1983 to 1985) pertain to Group II utilisations.

Note : OBA : Outside Bilateral Agreement.

per cent in 1981 (Sweden) and 1983 (USA). During 1984 only two markets reached the ceiling (USA and Sweden) as compared to three markets (USA, Sweden and Canada) in 1985. In the EEC there was not a single market where utilisations reached the upper limits in each of the six years under study. While it is true that aggregate quota utilisation has been low, does it mean that these quotas have not hurt India? The impact of quotas on Indian exports can be well seen in the category quota utilisations for USA and EEC over the same periods. In each sensitive category for USA the utilisation has been over 80 per cent during 1983, 1984 and 1985.[1] In respect of the EEC, utilisations have exceeded 80 per cent for categories 4,6, 15-B, 17, 26, 27 and 29 in some of the years (see Table 11). In some of these categories the utilisations have even exceeded 100 per cent. In respect of the EEC, category base levels are divided among EEC members in accordance with their burden sharing ratio. Hence, it is advisable to look at the category quota utilisations in respect of each EEC member country. Table 12 shows these levels in respect of sensitive categories. It will be observed that except in respect of some country/categories, utilisations are much below the 80 per cent level. This indicates that utilisation of quotas has been very inadequate in most EEC countries. Outside the EEC, Sweden and Canada are the two markets where utilisations have touched the ceilings in almost every category during last two years. Sweden, being a small market for India, has been absorbing imports very near the ceiling for India in five out of the six years under review.

Let us now try to examine the reasons for the inadequate utilisations in several country/categories. The reasons are sought in:

1. Administration of quota allocations.
2. Comparative advantages of the Indian apparel industry

## ADMINISTRATION OF QUOTA ALLOCATIONS

Do underutilised quota levels represent inadequate market demand for the products concerned? There are two aspects of this question. First, the nature of the QRs has been such that while some country/categories have been under 'effective' or binding restraints due to

[1] The rise in US dollar may have made the US market lucrative as compared with the EEC with reference to the given upper limits in the two markets.

Table 11

Category Quota Utilisations (percentage)

| Country/Category | 1980 | 1981 | 1982 | 1983 | 1984 | 1985 | 1986 | 1987 | 1988 |
|---|---|---|---|---|---|---|---|---|---|
| U.S.A. | | | | | | | | | |
| 334 | NS | NS | NS | NS | NS | 81.7 | – | – | – |
| 335 | NS | NS | NS | 107.4 | 96.7 | 97.8 | 104.04 | 62.47 | 95.02 |
| 336 | 96.6 | 89.0 | 84.6 | 112.7 | 94.4 | 97.0 | 102.97 | 126.67 | 118.13 |
| 337 | NS | NS | NS | NS | NS | 66.0 | 57.60 | 38.52 | 62.06 |
| 338–40 | 40.7 | 59.1 | 59.5 | 84.8 | 99.3 | 97.9 | 107.08 | 117.68 | 107.22 |
| 341 | 92.8 | 79.7 | 71.4 | 112.8 | 98.0 | 91.4 | 96.20 | 118.31 | 113.94 |
| 342 | NS | NS | NS | 109.5 | 104.2 | 97.7 | 109.16 | 124.61 | 114.54 |
| 347–48 | 91.9 | 114.1 | 91.7 | 111.8 | 102.9 | 94.6 | 114.76 | 125.05 | 105.85 |
| 350 | NS | NS | NS | NS | NS | 75.5 | – | – | – |
| 359 (J) | NS | NS | NS | NS | NS | 72.3 | – | – | – |
| 641 | – | – | – | – | – | – | – | 118.22 | 109.04 |
| Total Sensitive items | 78.1 | 75.6 | 69.5 | 105.3 | 98.8 | 94.1 | 100.76 | 116.52 | 110.85 |

Table 11 (contd.)

| Country/Category | 1980 | 1981 | 1982 | 1983 | 1984 | 1985 | 1986 | 1987 | 1988 |
|---|---|---|---|---|---|---|---|---|---|
| EEC | | | | | | | | | |
| 4 | 107.3 | 103.1 | 91.7 | 98.3 | 103.1 | 107.7 | 118.61 | 106.13 | 94.29 |
| 6 | 82.4 | 85.3 | 78.0 | 51.5 | 84.4 | 89.3 | 89.01 | 100.08 | 98.45 |
| 7 | 73.1 | 78.0 | 75.7 | 53.6 | 45.9 | 54.7 | 82.55 | 108.27 | 94.62 |
| 8 | 50.6 | 40.3 | 51.3 | 42.6 | 73.5 | 92.1 | 110.10 | 108.60 | 109.01 |
| 15–B | 85.2 | 73.8 | 68.7 | 43.0 | 51.5 | 53.8 | 50.44 | 67.67 | 62.57 |
| 17 | 87.2 | 28.7 | 16.9 | 27.4 | 24.8 | 20.5 | 28.73 | – | – |
| 21 | 14.5 | 17.1 | 12.8 | 13.3 | 16.2 | 18.8 | 26.40 | – | – |
| 25 | NR | 47.5 | 20.0 | 8.6 | 18.0 | 31.8 | – | – | – |
| 26 | 102.4 | 99.1 | 69.2 | 63.6 | 59.7 | 45.9 | 61.19 | 105.27 | 78.82 |
| 27 | 94.2 | 104.0 | 87.2 | 67.3 | 60.5 | 57.3 | 83.56 | 110.28 | 104.86 |
| 29 | 88.1 | 118.1 | 90.6 | 30.1 | 28.5 | 42.4 | 73.26 | 114.19 | 97.80 |
| 30–A | NR | 69.5 | 19.7 | 30.8 | 18.3 | 16.5 | 11.22 | – | – |
| 30–B | 4.5 | 4.1 | 1.4 | NR | NR | NR | – | – | – |
| 68 | NR | 0.0 | 0.0 | NR | NR | NR | – | – | – |
| Total | 71.0 | 68.2 | 65.0 | 58.9 | 61.2 | 69.1 | 88.79 | 106.79 | 96.98 |

Sources: 1) LS US Q No. 812 dt. 27.7.84.
2) LS US Q No. 3839 dt. 19.4.85.
3) Handbook of Export Statistics for Garments and Knitwear (1980-82), AEPC, New Delhi.

Note: NS: Non-sensitive
NR: Non-restricted

Table 12

Category/Countrywise Quota Utilisation (percentage)

| Year | All | 4 | 6 | 7 | 8 | 15-B | 17 | 21 | 24 & 25 | 26 | 27 | 29 | 30-A | 30-B | 68 |
|---|---|---|---|---|---|---|---|---|---|---|---|---|---|---|---|
| *Germany* | | | | | | | | | | | | | | | |
| 1980 | 82.8 | 115.5 | – | 110.3 | 40.7 | 97.3 | – | – | – | 111.4 | 104.7 | 89.2 | – | 1.8 | – |
| 1981 | 78.6 | 112.4 | – | 99.8 | 40.4 | 93.3 | – | – | – | 107.1 | 114.8 | 146.1 | – | 5.6 | – |
| 1982 | 73.2 | 93.5 | – | 91.6 | 46.8 | 97.7 | – | – | – | 85.9 | 91.2 | 89.3 | – | 2.5 | – |
| 1983 | 53.0 | 110.9 | 59.7 | 52.4 | 38.8 | 94.2 | 75.6 | – | – | 64.3 | 50.0 | 10.8 | – | – | – |
| 1984 | 54.8 | 116.4 | 102.5 | 40.2 | 47.5 | 114.2 | 55.5 | – | – | 53.2 | 56.8 | 17.3 | – | – | – |
| 1985 | 74.8 | 113.4 | 115.2 | 68.9 | 88.0 | 111.4 | 41.0 | – | – | 24.5 | 49.4 | 32.3 | – | – | – |
| *France* | | | | | | | | | | | | | | | |
| 1980 | 94.9 | 99.9 | N.R. | 100.6 | 85.8 | 102.2 | 95.8 | N.R. | – | 89.3 | 105.1 | 100.0 | N.R. | 7.8 | – |
| 1981 | 88.5 | 100.4 | – | 103.5 | 80.1 | 59.7 | 14.0 | 18.9 | 47.5 | 96.5 | 110.8 | 110.4 | 69.5 | 17.4 | – |
| 1982 | 72.0 | 90.1 | – | 94.0 | 48.5 | 46.1 | 1.7 | 10.6 | 19.0 | 77.5 | 94.2 | 91.9 | 19.7 | 4.0 | – |
| 1983 | 57.7 | 80.5 | 34.7 | 74.4 | 33.0 | 30.7 | 4.7 | 10.6 | 8.6 | 79.3 | 69.9 | 40.4 | 30.8 | – | – |
| 1984 | 59.9 | 105.5 | 61.3 | 66.4 | 57.7 | 27.9 | 1.7 | 12.0 | 8.0 | 72.2 | 57.4 | 35.5 | 18.3 | – | – |
| 1985 | 70.6 | 122.2 | 76.2 | 74.5 | 73.4 | 32.1 | 1.7 | 11.9 | 31.8 | 66.4 | 81.0 | 79.1 | 16.5 | – | – |
| *Italy* | | | | | | | | | | | | | | | |
| 1980 | 79.9 | 72.7 | N.R. | 82.6 | 82.6 | 50.0 | 77.6 | – | – | 87.9 | 81.0 | 47.5 | – | 0.0 | 0.0 |
| 1981 | 63.1 | 106.6 | 73.7 | 101.1 | 39.8 | 59.5 | 60.1 | – | – | 79.8 | 80.8 | 103.1 | – | 0.0 | 0.0 |
| 1982 | 44.9 | 92.7 | 43.7 | 96.1 | 7.8 | 70.9 | 55.0 | – | – | 61.9 | 73.1 | 103.0 | – | 0.0 | 0.0 |
| 1983 | 51.2 | 95.1 | 36.6 | 106.2 | 14.3 | 38.8 | 23.7 | – | – | 75.7 | 46.1 | 44.1 | – | – | – |
| 1984 | 40.0 | 76.4 | 45.8 | 68.2 | 24.4 | 11.8 | 3.9 | – | – | 42.1 | 22.7 | 22.3 | – | – | – |
| 1985 | 51.4 | 73.7 | 32.0 | 47.1 | 72.9 | 11.7 | 3.4 | – | – | 28.5 | 17.3 | 8.1 | – | – | – |

Table 12 (contd.)

| Year | All | 4 | 6 | 7 | 8 | 15-B | 17 | 21 | 24 & 25 | 26 | 27 | 29 | 30-A | 30-B | 68 |
|---|---|---|---|---|---|---|---|---|---|---|---|---|---|---|---|
| *Benelux* | | | | | | | | | | | | | | | |
| 1980 | 68.3 | 105.1 | 62.9 | 62.3 | 67.4 | 77.0 | 59.1 | 14.5 | — | 105.1 | 70.6 | 85.0 | — | 2.0 | — |
| 1981 | 62.4 | 102.0 | 86.8 | 64.7 | 45.6 | 80.7 | 32.0 | 16.1 | — | 86.4 | 91.4 | 125.6 | — | 0.0 | — |
| 1982 | 57.1 | 91.4 | 103.4 | 60.4 | 56.8 | 66.1 | 28.8 | 14.1 | — | 38.2 | 72.2 | 80.8 | — | 0.0 | — |
| 1983 | 42.9 | 110.1 | 67.8 | 30.2 | 52.8 | 34.3 | 15.0 | 14.8 | — | 20.7 | 44.9 | 30.7 | — | — | — |
| 1984 | 55.3 | 110.4 | 96.3 | 27.2 | 104.0 | 40.5 | 15.7 | 18.5 | — | 13.6 | 34.7 | 24.0 | — | — | — |
| 1985 | 66.3 | 122.0 | 97.7 | 40.2 | 121.8 | 41.0 | 18.3 | 22.6 | — | 12.9 | 33.8 | 56.3 | — | — | — |
| *Denmark* | | | | | | | | | | | | | | | |
| 1980 | 87.4 | 104.6 | — | 98.2 | 89.4 | 18.9 | — | — | — | 106.1 | 39.6 | 40.0 | — | 7.7 | — |
| 1981* | 86.6 | 111.7 | — | 104.5 | 77.0 | 54.7 | — | — | — | 93.9 | 44.1 | 73.3 | — | 0.0 | — |
| 1982 | 83.9 | 81.8 | — | 94.7 | 84.7 | 61.1 | — | — | — | 89.3 | 67.1 | 93.7 | — | 0.0 | — |
| 1983 | 76.4 | 99.0 | 101.5 | 85.0 | 58.7 | 65.6 | 20.0 | — | — | 67.2 | 93.9 | 38.7 | — | — | — |
| 1984 | 77.9 | 66.3 | 118.2 | 84.0 | 65.8 | 119.4 | 85.4 | — | — | 39.7 | 100.0 | 104.9 | — | — | — |
| 1985 | 89.1 | 71.9 | 105.0 | 104.0 | 105.2 | 84.3 | 61.7 | — | — | 31.5 | 83.8 | 95.6 | — | — | — |
| *U.K.* | | | | | | | | | | | | | | | |
| 1980 | 52.2 | 117.7 | 104.2 | 37.4 | 37.7 | 97.9 | 98.8 | — | — | 110.3 | 100.5 | 104.0 | — | 4.9 | — |
| 1981 | 55.0 | 95.9 | 102.7 | 54.3 | 32.4 | 90.1 | 28.7 | — | — | 108.7 | 112.6 | 108.6 | — | 2.9 | — |
| 1982 | 64.5 | 92.8 | 106.6 | 59.6 | 69.4 | 82.5 | 9.7 | — | — | 64.9 | 95.7 | 89.2 | — | 1.2 | — |
| 1983 | 56.6 | 96.9 | 47.7 | 47.3 | 54.7 | 113.9 | 2.8 | — | — | 66.0 | 102.1 | 45.2 | — | — | — |
| 1984 | 75.5 | 96.0 | 103.1 | 45.7 | 112.3 | 21.9 | 17.6 | — | — | 86.8 | 91.9 | 36.0 | — | — | — |
| 1985 | 68.3 | 108.8 | 106.7 | 40.8 | 96.7 | 30.1 | 18.6 | — | — | 71.2 | 74.3 | 40.7 | — | — | — |

Categories

Table 12 (contd.)

**Categories**

*Ireland*

| Year | All | 4 | 6 | 7 | 8 | 15-B | 17 | 21 | 24 & 25 | 26 | 27 | 29 | 30-A | 30-B | 68 |
|---|---|---|---|---|---|---|---|---|---|---|---|---|---|---|---|
| 1980 | 40.0 | 0.0 | – | 91.1 | 17.0 | 50.0 | N.R. | – | – | 93.3 | 36.8 | 100.0 | – | 5.9 | – |
| 1981 | 64.9 | 78.6 | – | 101.9 | 36.5 | 0.0 | N.R. | – | – | 135.3 | 45.2 | 100.0 | – | 0.0 | – |
| 1982 | 56.5 | 83.0 | – | 75.2 | 48.7 | 33.3 | 17.6 | – | – | 57.9 | 65.4 | 75.0 | – | 0.0 | – |
| 1983 | 51.8 | 45.6 | 8.1 | 90.6 | 51.6 | 0.0 | 0.0 | – | – | 52.2 | 38.7 | 22.7 | – | – | – |
| 1984 | 58.1 | 26.7 | 21.0 | 55.8 | 95.4 | 25.0 | 0.0 | – | – | 40.0 | 27.3 | 29.2 | – | – | – |
| 1985 | 68.0 | 43.7 | 82.5 | 61.3 | 94.5 | 11.1 | 0.0 | – | – | 96.3 | 48.6 | 11.5 | – | – | – |

*Greece*

| Year | All | 4 | 6 | 7 | 8 | 15-B | 17 | 21 | 24 & 25 | 26 | 27 | 29 | 30-A | 30-B | 68 |
|---|---|---|---|---|---|---|---|---|---|---|---|---|---|---|---|
| 1980 | – | – | – | – | – | – | – | – | – | – | – | – | – | – | – |
| 1981 | 66.7 | 48.0 | – | 76.4 | 36.0 | 100.0 | – | – | – | 100.0 | 77.8 | 350.0 | – | – | – |
| 1982 | 41.4 | 40.7 | – | 83.9 | 26.9 | 0.0 | – | – | – | 22.6 | 33.3 | 33.0 | – | 0.0 | – |
| 1983 | 37.2 | 07.5 | 12.0 | 94.0 | 27.3 | 42.9 | 15.0 | – | – | 42.0 | 36.8 | 52.6 | – | 0.0 | – |
| 1984 | 63.2 | 59.5 | 17.3 | 86.2 | 22.5 | 11.1 | 21.7 | – | – | 102.3 | 95.1 | 100.0 | – | – | – |
| 1985 | 76.3 | 01.9 | 3.7 | 113.9 | 100.0 | 66.7 | 7.7 | – | – | 139.1 | 113.6 | 108.7 | – | – | – |

*Norway*

| Year | All | 1 & 2 | 3 | 4 | 5 | 6 | 7 | 8 | 10 | 17 | 18 |
|---|---|---|---|---|---|---|---|---|---|---|---|
| 1980 | 27.8 | 94.9 | 109.9 | 95.4 | 50.0 | 74.1 | 99.7 | 97.1 | 23.7 | 95.0 | 95.6 |
| 1981 | 34.5 | 108.3 | 95.1 | 109.1 | 67.4 | 107.4 | 91.6 | 99.3 | 0.0 | 132.3 | 125.0 |
| 1982 | – | 0 | B | A | | | | | | | |
| 1983 | – | 0 | B | A | | | | | | | |
| 1984 | – | 0 | B | A | | | | | | | |
| 1985 | 96.1 | 108.1 | 121.2 | | 102.5 | 77.8 | 103.9 | 52.4 | – | – | – |

*Table 12 (contd.)*

| Year | All | 1 & 2 | 3 | 4 | 5 | 6 | 7 | 8 | 10 | 17 | 18 |
|---|---|---|---|---|---|---|---|---|---|---|---|
| **Sweden** | | *II* | *IV* | *V* | *VIII* | *IX* | *X* | *Rest* | | | |
| 1980 | 99.8 | 98.3 | 112.2 | 97.9 | — | 98.3 | 45.6 | 110.2 | | | |
| 1981 | 105.1 | 92.9 | 109.6 | 107.5 | 105.3 | 107.8 | 42.6 | 123.6 | | | |
| 1982 | 87.7 | 77.4 | 81.7 | 90.5 | 80.9· | 89.3 | 34.6 | 55.4 | | | |
| 1983 | 74.8 | 56.8 | 98.2 | 90.9 | 73.6 | 71.5 | 79.3 | 49.6 | | | |
| 1984 | 101.8 | 100.4 | 86.5 | 105.1 | 110.0 | 91.7 | 89.9 | 182.5 | | | |
| 1985 | 100.9 | 96.7 | 103.5 | 106.3 | 103.3 | 99.8 | 94.4 | 113.2 | | | |
| **Finland** | | *LB* | *GS* | *T.Shirts* | *Austria* | *All* | *LB* | *GS* | *Misc.* | | |
| 1980 | 72.0 | 69.8 | 77.0 | N.A. | | 70.3 | 105.5 | 36.4 | 68.7 | | |
| 1981 | 53.2 | 58.5 | 40.9 | N.A. | | 55.2 | 92.3 | 85.0 | 44.5 | | |
| 1982 | 76.7 | 89.2 | 17.7 | N.A. | | 67.6 | 111.1 | 80.9 | 58.3 | | |
| 1983 | 63.6 | 53.1 | 41.6 | 111.0 | — | 95.1 | 99.4 | 88.6 | — | | |
| 1984 | 54.4 | 48.6 | 61.9 | 98.0 | — | 89.3 | 86.0 | 94.4 | — | | |
| 1985 | 56.4 | 52.8 | 95.4 | 93.1 | | 88.6 | 75.1 | 109.0 | — | | |
| **Canada** | | *1* | *2* | *3* | *4* | *5* | *8* | | | | |
| 1980 | 68.6 | 22.5 | 80.7 | 31.3 | 144.2 | 31.2 | 64.0 | | | | |
| 1981 | 75.3 | 27.5 | 102.1 | 82.1 | 83.3 | 33.3 | 10.7 | | | | |
| 1982 | 63.3 | 72.5 | 81.3 | 70.3 | 86.3 | 13.3 | 0.0 | | | | |
| 1983 | 73.6 | 63.2 | 83.0 | 112.2 | 134.2 | 30.0 | 0.1 | | | | |
| 1984 | 98.9 | 108.7 | 107.2 | 110.7 | 144.2 | 99.7 | 29.6 | | | | |
| 1985 | 108.0 | 110.3 | 114.0 | 119.5 | 127.3 | 95.5 | 72.9 | | | | |

**Source:** Handbook of Export Statistics for Garments and Knitwear (1980–82) AEPC, New Delhi and AEPC unpublished statistical Tables 1983, 1984 & 1985.

**Note:** Underlined data represent categories where restrictions were binding during one or more part of the Quota year.

quota levels, several others have been 'ineffective' or 'non-binding', due to unutilised levels. Secondly, even in the 'ineffective' restraint levels underutilised quotas do not imply a lack of effective demand for the country/category concerned. There have been several country/categories where export orders could not be fulfilled by Indian firms during the year even when year-end data showed unutilised quotas.

The evidence of this phenomenon is not far to seek. As explained earlier there are broadly two systems of quota allocation—'closed' and 'open'. In the closed system, quotas are allocated on the basis of past performance in a given country/category at the beginning of a quota year. A very small portion is left 'open' for distribution during three quota periods of the year. Since fashion and consumer preference in import markets keep changing every year, there is no certainty that an export firm will get export orders from the same country/category. If it gets orders in another country/category it must seek an allocation under the 'open' system. Several firms having export orders backed by confirmed irrevocable letters of credit then compete in the open system for allocation of quotas on a FCFS basis. If on any day the demand for quota allocation exceeds the availability thereof, the allotments are made on the basis of a cut-off export price[2]. Firms having export orders on prices higher than the cut-off price stand to gain quotas. Invariably the cut-off prices are determined on a day when demand exceeds availability of the quota in the 'open' section. The result is that several firms whose export prices are lower than the cut-off price are refused quotas. Similarly firms obtaining confirmed orders after the date are also refused. The result is that unless additional quantities become available, the open section gets shut till the first day of the next quota sub-period during that year. Firms either have to cancel their orders or seek transfer of PP quotas for a consideration. The price at which transfers are made will depend on the supply and demand for these quota transfers which are legally possible. If the cost per unit of the exporter plus the price for the quota is below the price received in the export markets, export will take place otherwise orders are cancelled. The price demanded for a quota transfer will depend upon the sellers'

---

[2] Firms with prices below cut-off prices are not given quotas. Hence, firms tend to inflate their prices in order to go above the possible cut-off prices. Since each firm is bound to repatriate export revenues, none of the foreign exchange can be diverted to foreign illegal accounts.

expectations of a rising or a falling demand and the buyer's cost and demand expectations. The sellers invariably hold back their quotas for two reasons, first, the expectation that they themselves may get an export order in the relevant country/category. Second, the PP quota holder can hold on to the quota without fully utilising it till almost the end of the quota year.[3] The penalties for non-utilisation till 1986 were not heavy and almost every firm held on to its quota allocation till late in the year. At the fag end of the year unused quantities were surrendered and put on the open section. However, by that time export orders that could not be executed earlier have been cancelled due to non-availability of quota. At the same time year-end data show unutilised quotas.

It is not in all cases that cut-off-prices are determined. In a case where the quantum of quota sought is the same as that available, no cut-off prices are determined and quota is exhausted. In such cases all applicants coming after that day are refused allocation.

During the three years (1980, 1981 and 1982) the FCFS (contract reservation) section was used by exporters not having PP quotas to reserve quotas against the firm export contracts on a FCFS basis. In each of these three years the FCFS (CR) had a larger share than the FCFS (ready goods). From 1983 onwards FCFS(CR) was abolished and merged into a single open section termed FCFS (small orders). There were several exhausted country/categories in the three time periods of each of the quota years. A detailed examination of the period-wise data has shown that there were twenty-seven country/categories having less than fully utilised quotas in 1980 where exporters could not execute export orders at different times during the year. The number of such country/categories were twenty-two and fifty-eight in 1981 and 1982 respectively. Table 13 shows that there were varying levels of unutilised quotas at the year end in such categories.

Several contracts were cancelled by the exporters due to non-availability of quotas in the open section in each of these years. On the other hand, unutilised balances were available at the year end in each of these categories.

Till 1982 along with FCFS (CR), there was another open section

[3] See para 2, Garment Export Entitlement Policy, 1986, AEPC, New Delhi. During 1987 this requirement has been changed to 50 per cent utilisation by 30 April, 25 per cent by 31 July and 25 per cent by 30 September Unutilised balances would have to be surrendered and put on the open system. See para 4(i), Export Trade Control Public Notice No. 20-ETC (PN)/86 dated 6 October 1986.

**Table 13**

*Number of Country/Categories*

| Year-end levels | 1980 | 1981 | 1982 |
|---|---|---|---|
| 90–99% | 10 | 7 | 15 |
| 70–90% | 12 | 10 | 26 |
| Less than 70% | 5 | 5 | 17 |
| *Country/Category total* | 27 | 22 | 58 |

called FCFS (Ready Goods). FCFS (RG) was available to exporters who had confirmed orders, and goods against these orders were also ready for export shipment. In 1981 and 1982 20 per cent of the annual level in each country/category was allocated to this open section. In 1983, however, this open section was merged with FCFS (CR) to give a single open section—FCFS (small orders). In 1983 and 1984 FCFS (small quantities) was the only open section with an allocation of 35 per cent of annual base levels. Over 1985 and 1986 these allocations have shrunk 30 and 25 per cent respectively of base levels. During 1986 this FCFS allocation was being allotted in the ratio of 15:7:3 during the three quota periods of a quota year.

A detailed examination and data from 1981 to 1985 show that in each of the years there were several categories where utilisation did not touch the ceilings, and yet the overall restriction became binding at the firm level due to non-availability of FCFS (small order) quotas for export to the EEC and USA. Table 14 shows that there were varying levels of unutilised quotas at the year-end even while overall restrictions became binding:

**Table 14**

*Number of Country/Categories*

| Year-end levels | 1981 | 1982 | 1983 | 1984 | 1985 |
|---|---|---|---|---|---|
| 90–99% | 5 | 14 | 4 | 6 | 10 |
| 70–99% | 6 | ·8 | 3 | 2 | 4 |
| Less than 70% | 0 | 9 | 7 | 2 | 2 |
| Total: | 11 | 31 | 14 | 10 | 16 |

In 1982 there were thirty-one country/categories having under-utilised quotas where export orders could not be executed during one or more quota periods during the year. During the three years (1983, 1984 and 1985) the number of categories has been relatively low. This is so because quotas in respect of most EEC countries are heavily underutilised. Quotas in respect of USA are overutilised as Group II ceilings have been reached and such categories are excluded from the tally given herein.

The point that is being made here is that both FCFS (CR) and FCFS (SO) systems are part of the open section of quota allocation. If in any quota period of any quota year a firm is unable to execute an export order due to non-availability of quota on FCFS basis, QRs become binding even when year-end ceilings are not reached. Table 14 shows the country/categorywise quota utilisations where restrictions became binding at the firm level for one reason or the other (see underlined figures). This goes on to prove the hypothesis 1, viz., 'underutilised quotas may also restrict trade'.

It may be noted here that the QR is binding for a group of firms in the export industry. This is the group of firms which do not have PP quotas. Quotas have become fully binding on this sector of the industry, while for the other sector holding PP quotas, it may not be binding. Trade restrictions have emerged in a sector of the industry which has confirmed export orders due to built-in inflex-ibilities in the quota allocation mechanism. The nature of PP quotas is such that export firms do not have to produce export orders to get PP quota allocations. They can wait to receive an export order and failing to get confirmed export orders they can legitimately transfer their quota for a consideration. At the fag end of a quota period they can even surrender their quota. Even on the first day of a quota year PP quota is finished as it has been allotted to firms. However, shipments may take place from month to month during the quota year. The fact that year end balances show underutilisation in base levels points that firms holding PP quotas were unable to ship goods and hence surrendered their PP quotas. So whenever FCFS is fulfilled any time during the year and simultaneously year-end balances show underutilisation, trade is restricted as the restrictions become binding on an active sector of the industry. So far 'swing', 'carryover' and 'carry forward' provisions have not been used in any large measure to ease the restrictions of the type mentioned here.

## COMPETITIVENESS OF THE INDIAN
## APPAREL INDUSTRY

There are four cornerstones on which the competitiveness of the Indian apparel industry rests:

1. Availability of wide variety of cotton fabric and tailoring materials.
2. Abundantly cheap skilled workers for simple cut, sew and finishing operations.
3. Structure of the apparel trade and industry.
4. Product mix of the industry.

### Cotton Fabrics

The Indian textile industry provides a wide panorama of handloom, powerloom[4] or mill-made fabrics. The Indian textile complex is so diversified that thousands of varieties of cloth are available to suit the changes in consumer preferences and fashion.

The Indian segment of the world textile complex shows a striking departure from the textile industries of several national textile industries. The Indian textile complex differs from other national textile complexes as discussed in the following sections.

### ■ Number of Segments ■

We can view the world textile complex from the angle of three stages of processing—fibre stage, fabric stage and end-use stage. At each stage countries differ with respect to the number of segments of the industry. In India at each stage we have a unique decentralised sector. At the fibre stage we have the handspun fibre segment (khadi) along with the mill-spun fibre. At the fabric stage we have six different sectors—mills, powerloom, handloom, dyeing and finishing mills, khadi, hand-dyeing and finishing (see Figure 1). Each of these segments is quite independent and co-existent. In the end-use sector the basic uses are the same as in any country—industry, home furnishing and apparel. It is the apparel sector that is of prime interest to us. It has two segments— the factory type of readymade

---

[4] Mechanised and power driven looms in the decentralised sector outside the organised mill sector.

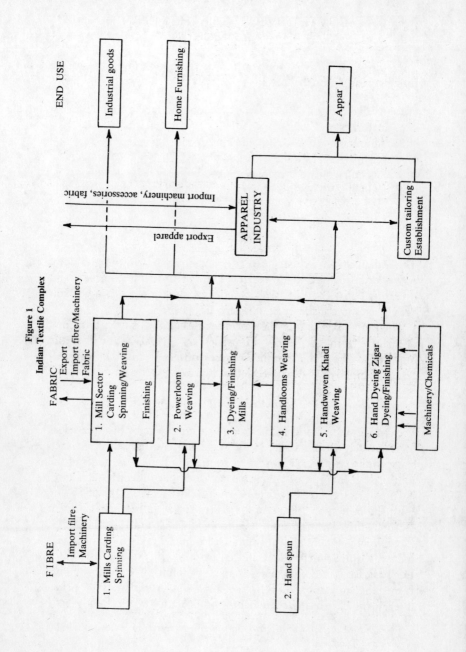

**Figure 1**
**Indian Textile Complex**

garment industry and the custom tailoring establishments. The latter dot every known retail market in the country turning out clothing made to measure to individual customer specifications.

### ▪ Degree of Integration ▪

Degrees of vertical integration differ significantly. Apart from a handful of firms in the mill sector most firms in the industry are highly specialised and confined to their stage of process. Vertical integration is almost non-existent in most parts of the industry. Horizontal integration is also an exception rather than the rule.

### ▪ Stage of Development ▪

A study (Walter, 1984) has tried to rank national textile industries according to six degrees of development, viz:

1. Embryonic stage
2. Export of native apparel
3. Increase in production of fabric and rise in apparel exports
4. The golden age of increasing sophistication and rising trade surpluses
5. Full maturity
6. Decline

If we were to place the Indian textile complex in the above format, the current stage of its development would correspond to the third stage mentioned previously. In this stage of its development the presence of a large decentralised sector provides a wide variety of fabrics and services that can meet the demand of the apparel industry. The linkages between the decentralised sector and the apparel industry are so strong that linkages between the mill sector and the apparel industry occupy a backbench position.

### ▪ The Cotton Edge ▪

The strength of the apparel industry rests on a steady supply of a wide variety of handloom, powerloom and mill-made fabrics of cotton from different segments of the Indian textile complex. The range of fabrics is so diverse that ready stocks of thousands of varieties can be procured by an apparel exporter. During 1985, 86.8 per cent of the total quantity of apparel exported to quota countries was made of cotton. This share has fluctuated between 85 per cent and 90.3 per cent during the period under reference. Table 15 shows that the quantum share of man-made fibre apparel was only 10.4 per cent in 1985, having slowly risen from 6 per cent in 1981. The share of woollen apparel has been negligible and declining since 1981.

Table 15

*Fibrewise Share of Apparel Exports to Sixteen Quota Markets (percentage)*

|  | 1981 | 1982 | 1983 | 1984 | 1985 | 1986 | 1987 | 1988 |
|---|---|---|---|---|---|---|---|---|
| Cotton | 88.0 | 85.0 | 90.3 | 89.3 | 86.8 | 82.15 | 85.90 | 84.57 |
| Man-made | 6.0 | 7.6 | 6.6 | 7.5 | 10.4 | 15.10 | 12.10 | 13.41 |
| Woollen | 6.0 | 7.4 | 3.0 | 3.1 | 2.7 | 2.75 | 2.00 | 2.02 |
|  | 100.0 | 100.0 | 100.0 | 100.0 | 100.0 | 100.00 | 100.00 | 100.00 |

The picture is more or less the same in respect of almost every market. Share of cotton apparel exported to each quota market (except Greece) fluctuated between 83.9 per cent to 97.8 per cent during 1985. In the case of Greece the share was between 83.9 per cent to 91.2 per cent during 1981 to 1984 and only in 1985 did it fall to 67.3 per cent, increasing the share of synthetic apparel to 30.9 per cent. This shift is insignificant in quantum terms as Greece is a very small market and a slight shift in fibre choice brings about a wide change of the sort observed in 1985.

It would not be off the mark to say that almost every firm in the industry targets its exports to the cotton apparel segment in these countries. The man-made fibre apparel exported from India should not be mistaken to be polyester based fabrics. A large part of man-made fibre apparel is rayon fibre based. Polyester based fabrics produced by the Indian textile industry are too expensive and internationally uncompetitive. For many years to come the strength of the Indian apparel industry is going to remain in the cotton apparels market. Some diversification may occur in cotton dominated blends, but internationally India's competing edge will be in cotton.

## Supply of Labour

The apparel industry is a labour-intensive industry where the amount of investment in fixed plant and machinery is very small (see Part II). The working capital requirements are many times the fixed costs even at increasing scales of operation. Direct labour costs account for a large chunk of total costs after material costs. The largest component of labour costs is in the form of skilled workers, such as, master cutters, tailors and other machine operators, and semi-skilled workers like overlock operators, button and hole operators, finishing workers like washermen, pressmen and packers. By and large production operations have remained non-mechanised. Only some operations in the production function have been semi-mechanised—these include cutting, embroidery, buttoning and overlocking operations with help of power-operated machines. The basic tailoring operation is by and large done on foot-operated sewing machines. There is an abundant and ever-expanding supply of skilled and unskilled workers. Workers have migrated from rural, semi-urban as well as other areas to flock to the apparel factories that have sprung up in and around large metropolitan areas of Bombay, Delhi and Madras. Wages are competitive and there is no scarcity of any type of workers.

## Structure of Trade and Industry

High labour intensity as a result of non-mechanised production operations has created a structure quite unique to this industry. This structure bears striking resemblance to the Italian apparel industry mentioned earlier. Notable features of its structure are: first, a broad base of thousands of firms specialising in different production operations localised mainly in Delhi, Bombay, Madras and some nearby towns. Since the bulk of the production is for export, localisation has concentrated in and around urban centres close to international airports from where the goods are exported.

Second, decentralised production operations dominate in cases where the more labour intensive production operations are sub-contracted to specialised firms known as 'fabricators'. Each exporter limits his own production operations to creativity intensive, quality control, materials supply, cutting, finishing, packing and shipping operations. Core tailoring operations are decentralised to several fabrication factories who work as sub-contractors to the exporter. In most cases fabricators are independent firms who perform sub-contracting jobs on the exporters' specifications. An exporter can sub-contract almost all his labour intensive production operations.

Third, this industry exhibits a phenomenon that we shall call 'economies of decentralisation'. Such economies result from central-ising operations that are less labour intensive, more mechanised and critical for product quality. As scale of operations can be achieved only by adding more workers, centralisation leads to dis-economies like rising overheads, overcrowding, and unionisation costs. So even small export firms tend to reap economies by decentralising the most labour intensive operations to other small firms. These result in substantial savings in unit costs of production and enhance the export competitiveness of the products. Since lead time even for large production runs is short and mostly seasonal, peak level employ-ment of workers on a full time basis for twelve months an year is not possible. Idle time costs would invariably push up unit costs if a firm were not to decentralise its operations. The decentralisation allows a fabricator to work for various export firms at different periods of the year. Some fabricators work only part of the year. They close shop during lean periods and ask the workers to return to their native places. The workers return when work resumes, this time bringing new workers with them. There are thousands of such fabricators in the city of Delhi alone.

Fourth, the entire apparel industry is an export-oriented industry. Very few firms are producing exclusively for the domestic market. The type of products exported have almost negligible home market due to differences in consumer preferences and clothing habits.


## Product Mix of the Industry

The export product mix of the industry is dominated by four types of garments which constitute normal western attire:

1. Ladies blouses and gents shirts
2. Ladies dresses
3. Ladies skirts
4. Trousers and shorts.

These four products represent the primary products of the Indian apparel industry and accounted for as much as 64.93 per cent and

69.98 per cent of India's total 1985 exports by quantity and value respectively to the sixteen quota countries. Table 16 shows the primary product specialisation of Indian apparel exports from 1980 to 1989. It will be observed that the primary product specialisation of the export sector of the apparel industry has declined by 15.48 per cent in quantity terms and 8.23 per cent in value over the period 1980–85. The reduction of the share of these primary apparel is an indicator of the increasing product diversification. There are over fifty different types of apparel items which India exports today, yet the export trade is dominated by these four basic types of apparel.

Table 16

*Primary Product Exports to Quota Countries (percentage)*

|          | 1980  | 1981  | 1982  | 1983  | 1984  | 1985  | 1986  | 1987  | 1988  | 1989  |
|----------|-------|-------|-------|-------|-------|-------|-------|-------|-------|-------|
| Quantity | 79.41 | 71.03 | 69.13 | 74.14 | 65.85 | 64.93 | 64.12 | 64.65 | 62.83 | 64.92 |
| Value    | 78.21 | 71.33 | 75.65 | 73.58 | 66.58 | 69.98 | 69.76 | 67.41 | 66.56 | 65.66 |

**Source :** Computed from AEPC Data

The reasons for the dominance of these types of apparel are the following: *First*, simple cut and sew operations are required for producing these kinds of apparel. Machines required are of similar types and skills compatible with those needed. Organisation of production operations is on similar lines and is capable of decentralised production. *Second*, since exports are dominated by cotton fabric which is meant for western summers, production runs are very short due to abrupt fashion changes. Such garments can be manufactured in large quantities even in short production periods. Specialised types of machinery and skills are needed for other garments like socks, jackets, gloves, cardigans, suits and gowns. Most production facilities are not equipped to handle such products, hence they confine their product lines to these four types of apparel mentioned above. It is not easy for firms engaged in producing primary products to employ their workers and machines to produce other items like jackets, sweaters, underwear, gents suits and coats. The very strength of the primary product specialisation of this industry also becomes its weakness because each of these products faces quota restrictions in almost all quota markets.

# 5

# Export Prices and
# Quota Rents

The economic impact of quantitative restrictions appears to influence the exporting as well as the importing country. One study of the US automobile industry, which is protected against Japanese imports by quantitative restrictions, examined the impact and suggested that it had resulted in raising Japanese export prices. It held that the US–Japanese VER agreement in respect of automobiles served mainly to shift imports to European sources, increase Japanese export prices and cause product upgrading by the Japanese automobile industry with accompanying increase in export prices (Kreinin, 1984). According to another study the economic effects of QRs can be divided into five categories (Hamilton, 1984):

1. Impact on production and consumption
2. Trade diversion effects within free trade areas and customs unions
3. Upgrading effects on commodity composition of trade
4. Rent from protection captured by exporters
5. Comparison of import quotas with export quotas

The quotas under VERs are a measure by which an importing country imposes a quota on foreign supply which is subject to five constraints:

1. There is an upper limit beyond which imports will not be allowed
2. The upper limit is broken down into each category of the product concerned
3. From the importing country's perspective the upper limit as well as category limits is defined by country of export
4. The limits are calculated by volume rather than value (number of pieces of apparel in our case). The limits correspond to a certain period (quota year) or several years (MFA period) divided into growth years.

The main basis on which such a quota differs from a tariff is that the latter is based on a commodity and is non-discriminatory (MFN) in application. A tariff is not defined by source and is normally levied on an MFN basis. Even a preferential tariff is rarely export country specific. However, it can be specific to a group of countries like GSP preference and ACP preferences. A tariff quota may be based on the quantity of imports but is not country specific and is also operated on an MFN basis. Such a tariff quota is operated on imports of apparel into Australia.

QRs create increased scarcity of imports and wholesale as well as retail prices of imports rise in the country. Somewhere along the chain linking the exporter and the retailer in the country of import this price increase is reflected in a premium added to the producer's price. According to a study (Deardorf and Stern, 18) if DD' be the logarithmic demand curve without quota $Q_0$ is imported at price $P_0'$ (see Figure 2). Once a quota $\hat{Q}$ is imposed, the demand curve changes to a kinked curve DABC. Given the supply curve SS', the world price will fall to $P_1$ in the case of a non-marginal supplier on the world market.[1] But since domestic demand is unchanged, domestic price rises to $\hat{P}$. $\hat{P}-P_0$ is the premium that emerges.

This explanation about quota premium ($\hat{P}-P_0$) is not free from defects. *First*, in the case of apparel quotas it is not the demand curve that gets kinked but the supply curve that develops a kink at B to give a restricted supply curve SBA. In fact the situation can be depicted either way. *Second*, for any quantity actually demanded in a quota period being below $\hat{Q}$ the price to the producer can actually fall below $P_0$. No quota premium emanates. *Third*, only if the quantity

[1] India is still a marginal supplier of apparel.

**Figure 2**
***The Price and Quantity Effects of a
Quota or a Variable Levy***

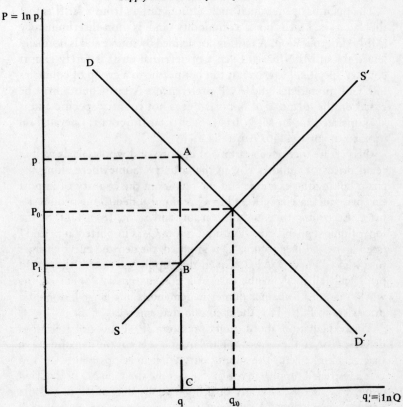

*Supply and Demand for Imports*

demanded in a quota year actually exceeds $\hat{Q}$ that $\hat{P}$ price will be paid with a quota premium of $\hat{P}-P_0$. One cannot assume that all QRs are binding and lead to quota premia. This situation can be easily seen with a kinked supply curve and shifting demand e.g. due to business cycle variation. There is considerable evidence to show that QRs cause rising prices only when the total quantity demanded in a quota period actually exceeds $\hat{Q}$. However, this study seeks to show that QRs can cause rising prices even at levels below $\hat{Q}$. The argument used earlier that due to a more complex situation in the supply side quota allocation system the price may go up in a sector of the export industry is not contradictory. During early 1986 US customs authorities were surprised to see different consignments of the same type and style of garment being shipped by different Indian exporters at widely varying FOB prices to the same importer. According to Indian trade sources, US customs placed some Indian firms under surveillance in early 1986 suspecting such price variations as being designed to evade customs duties. Such variations were actually due to higher prices for shipments made on FCFS quotas or transferred PPQs and lower prices on shipments made on PP quotas. An importer usually adjusts to the situation as he buys one style from several exporters holding different quotas at different FOB prices and usually adds his markup to the average price for the consignment as a whole. The effect of such a restriction even when the overall quota $\hat{Q}$ is not fulfilled is to raise prices in some of the import–export transactions emerging from the affected sector of the industry. Transaction-wise price analysis of sectoral data can reveal this. Unfortunately, such data were not available for this study.

Another study by Hamilton (Hamilton, 1984) proposes a similar explanation of quota rents. According to Hamilton, in a situation without a quota $OQ_0$ sells at price $P_0$ in the import market (see Figure 3). A VER (QR) restricts imports to $Q_2\,Q_3$ as a result of which the price rises to $P_1$ in the import market. For a non-marginal importer in the world, market price should fall to $P_2$. Domestic production rises to $OQ_2$ and imports fall to $Q_2\,Q_3$. Supply price remains at $P_2$ as the home country in this case is non-marginal, and difference between $P_1$ and $P_2$ assuming no tarriffs going as quota rent to exporter. This study goes on to say that one reason why exporting countries prefer this protectionist measure rather than tariffs or import quotas is due to the quota rents derived by the exporting country (Hamilton, 1984).

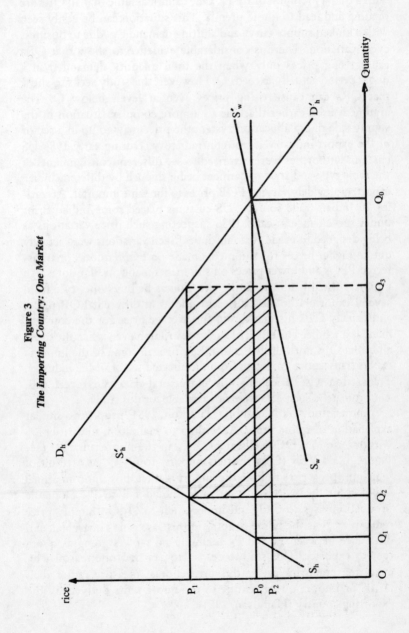

Figure 3
*The Importing Country: One Market*

This explanation of quota rents is open to question on the following counts:

1. Quota rents emerge in only those exporting countries where restrictions become binding at the firm level in one or more sectors of the export trade and industry. In countries where unexhausted levels are found and quotas are not binding at the firm level, quota rents do not occur.

2. Even in an exporting country having unexhausted base levels, quota rents may occur only in respect to categories or classes of goods where restrictions became binding at the firm level even below restricted upper limits. An inflexible quota allocation mechanism of an exporting country can create binding restrictions for export firms. In India's case such a situation has been created in the past.

3. In restrictions like the MFA quotas broken down countrywise as well as categorywise for each quota period, one cannot see the supply schedule as a single schedule. Rather it is a set of different supply schedules each representing an exporting country (or groups of countries). It can be seen as a single schedule only in the case of a global import quota.

4. Normally import penetration of an import market has begun with one or two countries (early entrants) who captured lion's share of the market. Quotas freeze these shares along with the minor shares of latecomers and newcomers. Over time (as over the first three MFAs) leading exporters may lose their initial competitive advantages as their comparative costs rise. In a free trade situation or even under global import quotas their shares would have fallen to newcomers or latecomers. But this does not happen under MFA quotas.

5. A global import quota can be represented by a single supply schedule and quota rents can occur only if the quota is binding at the firm level at import end. Quota rents may be cornered by the import trade. Such global import quotas will tend to have a depressing influence on f.o.b. export prices as compared to prices under MFA type QRs. However, under such a regime market shares of the exporting countries will reflect their dynamic comparative advantages. Some newcomers or latecomers will definitely improve their market shares to the extent they gain from shifts in comparative

advantage. Such a global import quota currently operates in Australia.

The MFA has resulted into a market sharing arrangement that has frozen shares in favour of early entrants. It has been attempted here to explain the situation with the help of more than one demand and supply schedules in eight different phases of the market situation, (see Figure 4).

## PHASES I AND II

A high income high consumption market has a competitive industry and no imports take place in Phase I. Lower cost imports from a group of countries make initial entry into the market and over some time gain a market share $= I_1$. As imports are allowed in Phase II, consumers will increase their consumption as the price falls. The overall supply (imports and domestic production) increase with imports taking a substantial share of the increase. The domestic production initially falls. Domestic industry begins to face import competition. In the case of apparel this phase is characterised by the Short-term Arrangement (see Figure 4).

## PHASES III AND IV

Since there is substantial unutilised capacity with foreign producers as well as supply of cheap skilled labour and other inputs, exporting countries are willing to supply even more at lower prices as larger orders generate more profits at the firm level. The process is accelerated with entry of latecomers who are willing to offer similar goods at lower prices. The supply schedule of early entrants $(E_1)$ tilts to supply more at lower prices. The supply schedule of latecomers $(E_2)$ targets itself near the lower end of the market to gain a foothold. It captures a share $(I_2)$ of the market and the share $(I_1)$ of early entrants also rises. Meanwhile the demand schedule shifts as the price falls further.

Phase IV is a continuation of the process as both early entrants and latecomers consolidate and expand their shares as import penetration rises. The foreign supply schedules $E_1$ and $E_2$ tilt further

**Figure 4**
*IMPACT OF MFA QUOTAS (Phases I to VIII)*

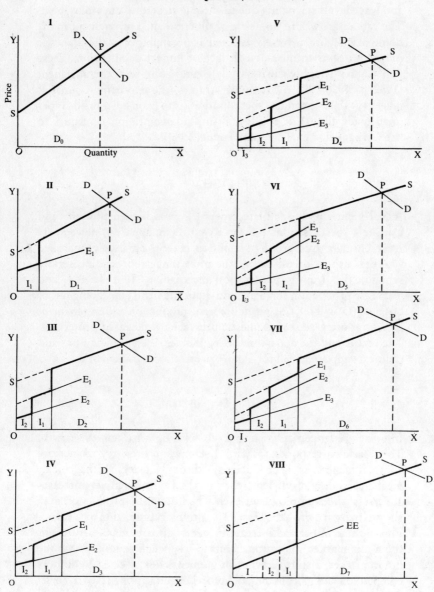

to supply even more at lower prices particularly when the export firm does not have to incur heavy overheads to expand capacity. There are no barriers to entry in the exporting country's industry and wage levels stagnating due to chronic structural unemployment. The rate of growth of domestic production and employment in the home market are adversely affected as profitability in the domestic industry begins to nose-dive in face of import competition. These two phases roughly correspond to the Long-term Arrangement (1962 to 1973). To overcome restraints, the exporting countries diversify their product specialisation into non-restrained types (man-made fibres) of goods and import penetration continues to rise (Arpans, De La Torre and Toyne, 1982).

## PHASE V

As early entrants $E_1$, and latecomers $E_2$ upgrade their products and gain new specialisations (cotton to synthetic apparels) newcomers representing a third group of countries enter the market as marginal suppliers at the lowest end of the price range representing supply schedule $E_3$. Import penetration increases to $I_1 + I_2 + I_3$ and domestic production stagnates and domestic firms start going out of business ($D_3 = DD_4$). Stagnant domestic production and employment in the industry sets up domestic pressure to increased protection. The textile and the apparel industry lobbies, their trade unions and political supporters call for a more protectionist framework.

## PHASE VI

Imports are frozen at existing levels with nominal annual growth. This phase corresponds to MFA-I. Domestic firms try to increase competitiveness and productivity through better management, mechanisation and efficient work methods. Productivity increases adversely affect employment even when domestic production may show a marginal growth ($D_5 \simeq D_4$). This is accompanied by a reduction in the number and increase in size of apparel manufacturers in the home market, a locational shift to low wage regions within the home market, a shift to types of garments less affected by import competition and globalisation of apparel manufacturing (De La Torre,

Jedel, Arpan, Ogram and Toyne, 1978). Protectionist sentiments continue as a result of falling employment and thus restrictions continue. MFA-I is extended into MFA-II. Prices begin to rise.

## PHASE VII

Domestic demand schedule has been rising to reflect natural growth. The foreign supply schedules $E_1$ and $E_2$ rise due to upgradation and quota premia based on binding restrictions. The foreign supply schedule $E_3$ does not rise due to substantially underutilised quotas. While quantity shares of $I_1$, $I_2$ and $I_3$ remain almost the same the value of exports from early entrants and latecomers is much higher due to higher prices. The market shares of newcomers ($E_3$) are small and the size of their export sector insignificant; quotas have little impact as they are not binding in most country/categories. Governments representing these countries do not seriously oppose continuation of MFA, nor do they seek any major reform in it. Pressures from newcomers are sought to be absorbed as a result of cutbacks from dominant suppliers among early entrants and latecomers. MFA is renewed to its third phase.

The apparel sector of the newcomers expands and quotas become binding in several country/categories. The share of these countries ($I_3$) expands to the upper limits of quotas. India as a newcomer experienced this phase during MFA-III in respect to its major export markets.

Thereafter, the upgrading effect combined with quota rents pushes up the value of exports while the quantity of exports more or less stagnates. Quantum market shares of early entrants ($I_1$), latecomers ($I_2$) and newcomers ($I_3$) more or less remain the same with $I_1$ and $I_2$ having lion's share of the market. Domestic production begins to expand with the natural growth of the market ($D_6 > D_5$). Domestic prices continue to rise.

## PHASE VIII

This is the phase that has begun in late 1986. A continuation of the MFA into its fourth term has prolonged the seventh phase into a stalemate where new entrants like India are deprived of market shares based on comparative advantage due to QRs. An alternative that was possible for developing countries to advocate is a regime of global quotas administered at the destination of export without any discrimination as to source of supply. A global quota for apparel in a country can specify the upper limit of imports that will be allowed in a market during a quota year. Competing exporters can capture market shares that reflect their country specific comparative advantages. Such a situation can be presented by a single global supply schedule. The result of a global quota will be that the supply schedules of dominant exporters among early entrants ($E_1$) and latecomers ($E_2$) will tilt in order to maintain their market shares in the face of global competition. Market shares of newcomers ($E_3$) who possess greater comparative advantage will expand. The general level of import prices will be subdued. This, however, is not to occur as MFA-IV will extend till 1991 and may be extended subsequently too.

In such a case if there are some very sensitive groups of apparel, a tariff quota can help absorb quota rents, should they occur. The biggest advantage will be that market shares of new entrants are likely to expand in the direction of their product specialisation. Larger market shares will then lead to product upgradation as a consequence of competition among exporting countries. Non-price competition will be particularly relevant for the purpose of product upgradation. Backward or forward vertical integration along the channels of distribution for branded goods will acquire significance in the marketing strategies of firms.

## EXPORT PRICES AND BINDING RESTRICTIONS

The hypothesis that is sought to be tested here is:

> *In respect of trade subject to QRs, quota rents in the exporting country occur in only those product categories exported to a specific country where restrictions actually become binding at the export firm level.*

In the context of MFA restrictions on global apparel trade, this hypothesis seeks to prove that quota rents do not arise as a natural consequence of QRs. They arise only when the restrictions imposed to protect home production and employment in an importing country become binding at the export firm level, i.e., where any individual firms along the channel of distribution are restrained for administrative reasons in any dimension of their natural business behaviour during the export–import transaction. Whether the restriction is administered at the export end or at the import end, as long as some firms are unable to carry out their business transactions with freedom quota rents will emerge. The surest way to test the hypothesis would be on the basis of quota prices in the market. Such data, however, require export market knowledge and a day to day follow-up on quota prices for each country/category. This has been attempted in Part II.

In this part the secondary data based methodology used to prove this hypothesis relies on an analysis of export prices of Indian apparel. Since quota restrictions are administered at the export end, a comparative analysis of export prices of product categories where restrictions became binding at the firm level with those that were not so binding is considered crucial. The hypothesis will stand proven if it can be shown that comparable export prices (FOB export prices may not be comparable because there are also other factors that may increase the price, like changes in import demand) of product categories subject to binding restrictions were higher than where they were not binding.

To overcome problems of comparability of prices the comparison is being made in respect of value added. 'Value added' is defined as the difference between the wholesale FOB export price and the floor price for the given product. The floor price of an apparel product in India is generally a price at which the simplest version of the product can be exported. It includes all production costs and normal business profits. An actual price realisation higher than floor price indicates a value addition that is the result of the following components:

1. Quota rents
2. Quota induced upgradation in product quality
3. Natural upgradation in product quality
4. Foreign exchange rate fluctuations
5. Inflation

Impact of foreign exchange fluctuations and inflation will be common to all products exported irrespective of the restrictions being binding or not. Therefore, the difference between the value additions in products subject to binding restrictions as compared to products where they were not binding will give us the impact of quotas in terms of quota rents and induced product upgradation.

Natural product upgradation may occur even in export products where restrictions are not binding. Such upgradation normally results from marketing strategy of firms. On the other hand, binding restrictions induce firms to realise higher unit values. One way of doing that is through quality and design improvement over and above what the firm would have done naturally in the absence of binding restrictions. In the apparel industry it implies use of better quality fabrics, better workmanship and diversification to high fashion segments of the market. Such upgrading has been mentioned in three studies. One study (Feenstra, 1984) split the price increase of Japanese cars imported into US in three components, viz., inflation, quota rents and quality improvement. It found that two-thirds of the price increase was due to quality improvements like longer and heavier cars, increased horsepower and automatic transmission systems. However this quality improvement was not necessarily demanded by consumers. Two other studies (Keesing and Wolf, 1980), (Lin and Mok, 1980) also mention such upgrading in the context of the textiles and apparel industries as a cause for rising export prices.

For the purpose of our analysis we can look at two aspects of prices. *First*, unit value added in binding product categories $(V_n)$ as compared to unit value added in non-binding categories $(U_n)$ during a quota year for a given country market. *Second*, we can analyse the increase in value added $(V_n)$ on a time-series basis for a given country/category as a result of binding restrictions. Such an analysis will give us the combined impact of quota rents as well as induced product upgradation $(V_n - V_{n-1})$ the difference between unit value added in an year when restriction was not binding $(V_{n-1})$ and the year when it became binding $(V_n)$ will give us the impact of quotas. The difference $(V_{n+1} - V_n)$ or $(V_{n+2} - V_{n+1})$ (where $V_{n+2}$ and $V_{n+1}$ are subsequent years when quotas continue to be binding) will represent variations between the intensity of restrictions based on demand conditions.

Where:

$(V_{n+1} - V_n) = 0$ represents no change in demand and no inflation.[2]
$(V_{n+2} - V_{n+1}) > 0$ represents relative increase in demand.
$(V_{n+2} - V_{n+1}) < 0$ represents relative decrease in demand.

Also: $V_n - U_n = P_n$ (Price impact of quotas)
$TP_n = P_n \times Q$ (Total price impact of quotas).

[2] We can also take ratios (percentage) so that inflation can be accounted for.

During 1983–85 there was only one open section of quota allocation, i.e., FCFS. If firms were unable to get quota on FCFS they had to buy it on the free market at a possible price. Since in almost every market the first two quota periods are the peak business periods for Indian exporters, non-availability of quota during these periods implied that the restrictions became binding at the firm level thus inducing quota rents. The size of the rents would however depend on the size of the demand relative to the availability of quotas. We can analyse these factors in the context of the US market which is India's largest single market.

USA is the largest single market for Indian apparel. The Indian bilateral agreement with USA during MFA-III, has been most restrictive in its character. In addition to quotas, there was a Group II overall ceiling for all apparel categories. The result was that during 1983 and 1984, 96 to 98 per cent of Indian apparel exports to the US fell under binding restraints. These quotas were available to firms during a twelve month accounting period. Daily movement of quota distribution shows that in the open segment (FCFS) of quota allocation, business firms were effectively restrained for most part of the year. Table 17 gives the number of days for which firms were restrained from confirming contracts for export of woven apparel due to non-availability of quotas (FCFS).[3]

**Table 17**

*Number of Days Restrained: US Quota Categories*

| US Categories | 335 | 336 | 338–40 | 341 | 342 | 347/48 |
|---|---|---|---|---|---|---|
| 1984 | 363 | 363 | 223 | 341 | 363 | 363 |
| 1985 (Jan.-Oct.) | 294 | 281 | 301 | 302 | 286 | 279 |

**Source :** AEPC

The US government imposed unilateral restrictions on seven apparel categories in 1984. Only two of them were withdrawn following recommendation of the Textile Surveillance Body. In each case the Indian side felt that there was hardly any data to prove a case of market disruption or threat thereof in terms of Annex A of

[3] Even if these are a small number of categories in one fibre type, they are precisely areas where Indian firms have export capabilities and are subject to QRs.

MFA. The imposition of restraint levels on non-restrained categories appeared in conjunction with the Group II ceiling to exacerbate the undesirable impact of these quotas on the Indian apparel industry.

US quotas became binding in most sensitive categories for the first time in 1983 and the same trend continued in 1984 and 1985. Table 18 shows unit value added for each category during 1981 to 1985.

**Table 18**

*USA:  Unit Value Added ($V_n$)*
*(Rs. per piece)*

| Category | Years | | | | |
|---|---|---|---|---|---|
| | 1981 | 1982 | 1983 | 1984 | 1985 |
| 334 | – | – | – | – | 33.34 |
| 335 | – | – | 9.38 | 24.79 | 20.86 |
| 336 | 16.68 | 18.48 | 18.35 | 30.37 | 26.51 |
| 337 | – | – | – | – | 29.76 |
| 338–40 | 7.23 | 9.18 | 11.07 | 15.63 | 21.77 |
| 341 | 3.53 | 4.41 | 3.80 | 12.96 | 13.08 |
| 342 | 7.62 | 9.86 | 6.08 | 22.09 | 24.29 |
| 347–48 | 9.50 | 26.39 | 1.29 | 20.88 | 21.25 |
| 350 | – | – | – | – | 48.85 |
| 359(J) | – | – | – | – | 9.93 |

**Source:** Computed from AEPC Data

It will be observed that these values for each category have increased at a faster rate during the three years, i.e., 1983, 1984 and 1985. The price impact of quotas for US market has been computed in Tables 19, 20 and 21. According to Table 19 the price impact of quotas ($P_n = V_n - U_n$) was Rs. 6.1 per unit during 1983. Total price impact of US quotas in 1983 works to Rs.137.1 million on the basis of 22,476,000 pieces of garments subject to binding restrictions in 1983. The computation for 1984 and 1985 is shown in Tables 20 and 21 respectively. Since there were no categories during 1984 and 1985 where restrictions were not binding, value of $U_n$ has been assumed to be the same percentage to average price as in 1983. These computations show that apparel exporters earned a total of Rs. 574.166 million and Rs. 614.71 million due to the impact of US quotas on Indian export prices during 1984 and 1985 respectively. Since these quota rents occurred only in binding categories our hypothesis is also proven. This burden was directly borne by the importers in

USA as a result of the higher prices prevailing in the US domestic markets for these type of apparel. Needless to say it ultimately reflected in higher consumer prices borne by the lower income segments of the US market.

Table 19

*Price Impact of US Quotas (1983)*

| Category | Binding | | |
| | $V_n$ (Rs.) | $TV_n$ ,000 Rs. | Q ,000 Pcs. |
| --- | --- | --- | --- |
| 335 | 9.38 | 15,716.95 | 1,675 |
| 336 | 18.35 | 58,549.52 | 3,191 |
| 338–40 | 11.07 | 120,024.18 | 10,840 |
| 342 | 6.08 | 24,841.53 | 4,086 |
| 347–48 | 1.29 | 3,466.94 | 2,684 |
| Total | 9.9 | 222,599.12 | 22,476 |
| Net Binding $U_n$ (Rs.) 341 | 3.80* | 119,954.6 | 31,567 |
| $(P_n)$ Price Impact | 6.1 | | |
| $(TP_n)$ Total Price Impact | 6.1 | | 22,475 = Rs. 137.10 m. |

**Source:** Computed from AEPC Data.
* Works to 13.2 per cent of average price/unit in the category.

Table 20

*Price Impact of US Quotas (1984)*

| Category | $V_n U_n P_n$ (Rs.) | $Q_n$ (Rs.) | $TP_n Q_n$ (Rs.) | Binding | |
| | | | | $Q_n$ , 000 Pcs. | $TP_n$ , 000 (Rs.). |
| --- | --- | --- | --- | --- | --- |
| 335 | 24.79 | 8.26 | 16.53 | 1599 | 26431.47 |
| 336 | 30.37 | 8.86 | 21.51 | 2861 | 61540.11 |
| 338–40 | 15.63 | 4.49 | 11.14 | 13083 | 145744.62 |
| 341 | 12.96 | 4.35 | 8.61 | 28260 | 243318.60 |
| 342 | 22.09 | 7.22 | 14.87 | 4121 | 61279.27 |
| 347–48 | 20.88 | 7.31 | 13.57 | 2642 | 35851.94 |
| Total | | | | 52,566 | 574166.01 Rs. 574.166 m. |

**Source:** Computed from AEPC Data.

Table 21

Price Impact of US Quotas (1985)

| Category | Binding | | | | |
| --- | --- | --- | --- | --- | --- |
| | $V_n$ (Rs.) | $U_n$ (Rs.) | $P_n$ (Rs.) | $Q$ '000 Pcs | $TP_n$ '000 Rs. |
| 334 | 33.34 | 10.34 | 22.00 | 327 | 7,194.00 |
| 335 | 20.86 | 8.68 | 12.18 | 1,714 | 20,876.52 |
| 336 | 26.51 | 9.41 | 17.10 | 3,143 | 53,745.30 |
| 337 | 29.76 | 8.55 | 21.21 | 593 | 12,577.53 |
| 338–40 | 21.77 | 6.74 | 15.03 | 13,278 | 199,568.34 |
| 341 | 13.08 | 5.42 | 7.66 | 27,129 | 207,808.14 |
| 342 | 24.29 | 8.42 | 15.87 | 4,095 | 64,987.65 |
| 347–48 | 21.25 | 8.66 | 12.59 | 2,599 | 32,721.41 |
| 350 | 48.85 | 12.39 | 36.46 | 154 | 5,614.84 |
| 359 (J) | 9.93 | 7.25 | 2.68 | 1,031 | 2,763.08 |
| 359 (V) | 45.90 | 35.88 | 10.02 | 191 | 6,853.08 |
| Total | | | | | 614,709.89 = Rs. 614.71 m. |

Source : Computed from AEPC Data.

Based on these computations we can state that 6.1 per cent, 19.7 per cent and 17.7 per cent of the value of exports to the US during 1983, 1984 and 1985 respectively was the result of QRs imposed on Indian exports. If values of $TP_n$ are expressed as a percentage of value of exports less $TP_n$, we get the export tariff equivalent of US quotas in the three respective years: 6.5 per cent, 24.5 per cent and 21.6 per cent. The only difference with these tariff equivalents is that this value went to neither the Indian nor the US governments but to Indian export firms having quota allocations. These equivalents compare well with the magnitudes and fluctuations estimated in another study (Hamilton, 1986). Hamilton's estimates are worked out on the basis of CIF import prices and therefore, he refers to them as import tariff equivalents. Our estimates are based on f.o.b. export prices which exclude insurance and freight (which may be about 7 to 10 per cent of f.o.b. value depending on the size of the shipment). Our estimates based on f.o.b. export prices are therefore referred to as 'export tariff equivalents'.

Hamilton estimated that the big-three apparel exporters, South Korea, Taiwan and Hong Kong, earned quota rental income of US $ 812 to 909 million (1985 prices) on exports of apparel to the USA during 1982-83. This was directly attributable to QRs under the MFA. Our estimates for India show that quota rent income derived by Indian firms was about $ 102 million during 1983 to 1985.[4] This was much lower than each of the estimates of incomes derived by the big-three apparel exporters.

These export tariff equivalents in fact influence only apparel exports subject to binding restrictions. Their strength, however, varies from category to category because of variations in demand intensity. Where restrictions became binding for only a part of the quota year, annual data may not clearly exhibit the impact of quotas on export prices. US quotas have been binding for most part of the year for categories included in the computations for 1983 to 1985 and the impact of quotas is clear.

A deeper insight into quota rents can come from detailed examination of different sectors of the export industry, the coverage of binding restrictions in terms of product categories, quantities and time periods for which they remain binding. Hamilton assumes that quota rents, once emerging in the form of quota prices, are applicable across the board to all quantities traded in the relevant year. This may not be so because quota prices may not affect export prices of all the firms in the industry, particularly when restrictions are binding only for part of the year or when they affect only one sector of the industry. The behaviour of quota rents, quota prices and quota markets is dealt with in detail in Part II.

[4] US $ = Rs. 13

# PART II

# RESPONSE OF APPAREL
# EXPORTING FIRMS

# 6

# The Sample and Methodology

The cultural environment of the Indian market is different from the cultural environments of most developed market economies which import Indian apparel today. The clothing habits of Indian consumers conditioned by the cultural environment are vastly different from western clothing habits. The type and styles of ethnic clothing sold in Indian markets constituting home demand for clothing are, therefore, not comparable with similar demand for clothing in the developed market economies. Indians consume vast quantities of custom-tailored clothing, manufactured in hundreds of thousands of small tailoring shops which dot every village, town and city bazaar. It was only during the 1960s that organised factory-made ready-to-wear clothing referred to as apparel or readymade garments began to grow in large metropolitan centres like Bombay and Delhi. Its product range was limited to western attire like ladies blouses and dresses, skirts, shirts and pants. The local market for such apparel was confined to a very small section of the urban population. Organised factory production began and grew up entirely in the small-scale industry sector. Consumers within the urban sector who wore western attire were and still are accustomed to made-to-measure clothing as compared to readymade garments. Hence, the evolution and growth of the apparel industry in India was almost entirely based on export demand. During 1965–66 there were only 120 firms exporting apparel, accounting for an export turnover of Rs. 63.83 million. By 1976–77 their number had risen to 3,929 (by 33 times) accounting for an export turnover of Rs. 2,625.5 million. Table 2 in the introduction shows that increase in the number of exporting firms had been accompanied by an increase in export turnover of about 40 times. Increase in apparel exports continued during MFA-II (1978–81). However, there was no corresponding increase in the number of export firms during this period. Indian apparel exports had been rising during the phase of LTA, MFA-I and MFA-II when QRs were generally not binding in most country/categories. It was only during MFA-III that QRs became binding in some country/categories. The increase in apparel exports was briefly arrested during 1982 and 1983, the first two years of MFA-III. However, since 1984, exports have been growing. Apparel exports crossed the Rs. 10,000 million, Rs. 13,000 million and Rs. 18,000 million marks in 1985, 1986 and 1987 respectively. The growth during MFA-III was under a quota regime which was only partially binding in macroeconomic terms. QRs were not binding in every export destination and every product category. During this period the number of export firms almost doubled—an addition of 4,087 firms between 1983 and 1986.

Economic statistics pertaining to the firms in this industry are almost non-existent. The only statistics that are available pertain to the export turnover of the industry (Lok Sabha, unstarred question 4689, dated 24 August 1984). An indication about the current size of this industry is based on the number of export firms and export turnover given in Table 2.

## STRUCTURE AND LOCALISATION

The industry has become localised in and around three metropolitan centres: Delhi, Bombay and Madras. These three centres accounted for 84 per cent of quantity and 89 per cent of value of apparel exported from India in 1987.

Table 22 shows Delhi has always been the top contributor to apparel exports followed closely by Bombay and Madras. Localisation of the apparel export industry in these three centres has been partly influenced by reasons of proximity to international airports in these three metropolitan cities since a bulk of exports are transported by air. Almost the entire production originates from these three centres. Small and large factories are located in industrial and suburban areas, slums and even urban villages located in and around the three cities. The share and significance of other centres like Tirupur and Ludhiana (for knitwear), Bangalore, Jaipur and Calcutta are comparatively small.

Table 22

Regionwise Origin of Indian Apparel Exports
(Quantity (Q) and Value (V) percentage showing contribution
of a region to national exports)

| Region | 1981 | 1982 | 1983 | 1984 | 1985 | 1986 | 1987 |
|---|---|---|---|---|---|---|---|
| Delhi Q | 38.33 | 36.12 | 37.70 | 39.49 | 35.01 | 33.21 | 35.08 |
| (V) | (48.24) | (44.43) | (45.06) | (45.09) | (42.03) | (39.96) | (41.72) |
| Bombay Q | 47.97 | 45.89 | 36.91 | 39.65 | 39.92 | 38.81 | 36.27 |
| (V) | (38.89) | (42.53) | (37.03) | (38.25) | (39.06) | (40.08) | (36.38) |
| Madras Q | 7.82 | 10.91 | 11.85 | 10.64 | 12.06 | 11.88 | 12.59 |
| (V) | (5.67) | (6.02) | (9.10) | (9.75) | (10.84) | (10.37) | (10.94) |
| Tirupur Q | n.a. | 0.48 | 7.09 | 4.52 | 6.73 | 9.60 | 9.01 |
| (V) | n.a. | (0.11) | (2.00) | (1.14) | (1.75) | (2.83) | (4.01) |
| Bangalore Q | 4.47 | 4.05 | .4.44 | 4.37 | 4.82 | 4.90 | 4.72 |
| (V) | (4.17) | (4.36) | (4.86) | (5.12) | (5.38) | (5.79) | (5.68) |
| Calcutta Q | 1.53 | 1.97 | 1.40 | 0.97 | 1.13 | 1.09 | 1.45 |
| (V) | (1.39) | (1.56) | (1.05) | (0.61) | (0.47) | (0.32) | (0.36) |
| Jaipur Q | 0.88 | 0.64 | 0.60 | 0.35 | 0.39 | 0.51 | 0.88 |
| (V) | (1.64) | (1.00) | (0.82) | (0.44) | (0.48) | (0.65) | (0.91) |
| All India Q* | 199009 | 186980 | 193440 | 230549 | 255949 | 300822 | 370116 |
| (V)* | (6500242) | (6335746) | (6401335) | (8501002) | (10676520) | (13231238) | (18574364) |

* Q in '000 pieces and (V) in '000 Rupees.

Source: Apparel Export Promotion Council, New Delhi.
Statistical Tables for 1980 to 1987.

Table 23 shows that 91.4 per cent (7,569) of export firms registered with Apparel Export Promotion Council in April 1986 were classified as merchant-exporters. Only 693 firms (8.4 per cent) were classified as manufacturer-exporters. This shows a very peculiar pyramid structure of the export trade and industry. Prima facie it exhibits a very narrow manufacturing base and a predominant trading network. Discussion with trade associations revealed that the actual number of organised manufacturer-exporters would be about 450 being recognised as such by the Textile Commissioner of the central government. As a result the organised manufacturing sector of the industry is very small. Trade sources estimate that about 1,000 of 7,569 merchant-exporters are regularly and actively involved in exports. An estimated 1,350 firms of both types account for 80 to

90 per cent of total apparel exports from India. Two questions that arise here are: First, where is the bulk of the export production undertaken? Second, what is the role of over 6,900 registered exporters who account for a marginal share of national exports? Both these questions are answered in the subsequent sections. At this point it will be sufficient to state that only about 1,350 export firms located in and around Delhi, Bombay and Madras account for the lion's share in Indian exports.

Table 23

*Regional Dispersion of Registered Apparel Exporters*
*(as in April 1986)*

| Region | Manufacturers | Merchants | All |
|--------|---------------|-----------|-----|
| Northern | 332 | 4453 | 4785 |
| Western | 182 | 2046 | 2228 |
| Southern | 160 | 960 | 1120 |
| Eastern | 19 | 110 | 129 |
| All | 693 | 7569 | 8262 |

**Source:** List of Members and Registered Exporters Apparel. Export Promotion Council, New Delhi April, 1986.

## THE SAMPLE SIZE AND TYPE

The sample for this study consists of 177 firms which responded to a two-phased survey. In the first phase a structured questionnaire was conducted by mail and aimed at chief executives of 1,000 firms located in Delhi, Bombay and Madras. Even though prior support of the industry's three trade associations[1] and the semi-official Apparel Export Promotion Council had been obtained, the mail response was only 0.04 per cent. Only four incomplete questionnaires were returned. In the first phase during late 1986 all eighty-five respondent firms had to be interviewed personally. Their selection was invariably based on their willingness to cooperate, hence the sample can be termed as a convenience-cum-judgement sample. The average length of the interview was between 40 to 60 minutes involving more than one visit to a respondent firm. Preliminary conclusions

[1] Garment Exporters Association (GEA)
   Clothing Manufacturers Association of India (CMAI)
   Apparel Exporters and Manufacturers Association (AEMA)

were based on the first phase sample of eighty-five firms and a preliminary report was completed in February 1987. However, it was felt that the size of the sample was small and the preliminary conclusions drawn on the basis of the first phase sample required support from a larger sample of firms. Consequently in the second phase during early 1987 an abridged structured questionnaire was used to personally interview another ninety-two firms. The analysis and results herein are based on the combined sample of 177 firms covered in both the phases of the survey.

The sample of 177 firms is actually composed of sub-samples for the purpose of our comparative classification. This classification divides the firms under study on the basis of impact of quotas, size, growth and geographic regions. In such a situation the number of degrees of freedom involves $(n_1 + n_2 - 2)$ which is large enough to permit the use of normal distribution. Hence, the Z test is applied to test the significance of the difference of means/proportions of a variable observed in sub-samples where appropriate. This is based on the assumption that our sample is a random sample.

## Sample Profile

The 177 firms in the sample accounted for a combined turnover of Rs. 2,815.7 million which constituted 21.3 per cent by value and 22.04 per cent by volume (66.3 million pcs) of Indian apparel exports during 1986. They represented about 13.1 per cent of the estimated 1,350 firms regularly involved in apparel exports. The sample is considered fairly representative of the industry.

For the purpose of comparative analysis of the firms represented in the sample we are using the following three classifications:

1. *Quota and Non-Quota firms*: A firm exports to quota as well as non-quota destinations. Within quota destinations it exports quota items as well as non-quota items (outside QRs). The impact of quotas is felt mainly on the sale of quota items to quota destinations. A firm whose exports of quota items were accounted for by over 61 per cent (i.e., over three-fifth) during the terminal year of the reference period was classified as a quota firm. This implied that such a firm had a major share of quota items in its product line, and to that extent it was influenced by the quota regime. Of the 177 firms 83.6 per cent (i.e., 148 firms) in the sample are classified as quota firms. Only twenty-nine

firms (i.e., 16.4 per cent) are classified as non-quota firms. The non-quota firms are intended to serve as a control group.

2. *Small and Large firms*: An export firm having a turnover of over Rs. 10 million in the terminal year of the reference period is classified as a large exporter. All firms having a turnover of Rs. 10 million and less are classified as small exporters. There are 103 large firms, i.e., 58.2 per cent, and seventy-four, i.e., 41.8 per cent small firms. The cut-off point of Rs. 10 million in turnover is based on the popular notion in India that an enterprise having an annual turnover of over Rs. 10 million cannot be considered small. Even under Indian corporate laws a private company was deemed to be a public company if its turnover exceeded Rs. 10 million which was considered 'large'.

3. *Growth and Non-Growth firms*: The reference period for the study is 1980 to 1986. A firm which has grown in terms of either quantum or value of turnover in the terminal year of the reference period as compared to 1980 is classified as a growth firm. A firm whose quantum and value of turnover in the reference period has either remained stagnant or declined has been classified as a non-growth firm. Out of the total 177 firms 140 (i.e., 79.1 per cent) are growth firms while thirty-seven firms (i.e., 20.9 per cent) are non-growth firms.

## Ownership

The ownership pattern of these firms reveals that 26 per cent (forty-six firms) operate as sole proprietorships, 5.1 per cent as partnerships and 68.9 per cent as companies with limited liability. Table 24 shows that the nature of ownership has very little to do with the size of the enterprise since corporations with limited liability dominate both large and small enterprises. Partnerships are least popular among small as well as large firms. This pattern is found in all three geographical regions—Delhi, Bombay and Madras.

## Age and Experience of Enterprises

Table 24 shows that 80.8 per cent of the firms have entered apparel exports during the three regimes of MFA. The largest number (33.9 per cent) entered the trade during MFA-III followed by 23.2 per cent during MFA-II and 23.7 per cent during MFA-I. Only 19.2 per cent of the firms have been in the trade prior to MFA (i.e., 1973 or before). This indicates the recent origin of the Indian apparel trade and industry. It also shows that the increase in apparel exports experienced during MFA has been largely due to entry of new firms in this sector. Any future slow-down in the entry of new firms or effective barriers on their entry into this sector may not be conducive to the growth of the apparel exports from India.

## Value of Turnover

Table 25 shows that the average value of turnover was Rs. 16.76 million per firm with the range between Rs. 0.1 million to Rs. 180 million. Classified by size, small firms showed an average export of Rs. 3.95 million as compared to Rs. 35.6 million for large firms and this difference was significant at a 1 per cent level of significance. Quota firms which were larger in number showed an average turnover of Rs. 15.3 million per firm which was lower than the average turnover of Rs. 24.4 million per firm for non-quota firms. This difference was, however, statistically insignificant. The growth firms showed an average of Rs. 19.1 million as compared to Rs. 7.9 million for non-growth firms. This difference was also significant at a 1 per cent level of significance. Among the regions, the firms in Delhi are the smallest in their average turnover which stood at Rs. 12.4 million as compared to the Bombay firms which had an average turnover of Rs. 33.7 million. This difference in sales per firm was significant at a 1 per cent level of significance. The higher sales of Rs. 22.5 million among Madras firms are significantly different from that of Delhi firms at a 10 per cent level of significance.

## Quantum of Turnover

The average quantity turnover was 4,17,000 pcs per firm with the range between 3,000 pcs and 5 million pcs. Table 26 shows that in quantity terms small firms sold 84,000 pcs as compared to 8,51,000 pcs in case of large firms. Quota firms sold 3,54,000 pcs as compared to 7,39,000 pcs by non-quota firms but this difference was not significant. Growth firms sold 4,54,000 pcs as compared to 2,70,000 pcs in case of non-growth firms. This difference was statistically significant at a 1 per cent level of significance. The quantity sold by Bombay firms was significantly higher than that of Delhi firms (at the 1 per cent level).

**Table 24**

*Number of Firms in Sample*

| Nature Ownership | Year of Commencement-MFA | | | | Growth | | Quota | | Size | | Region | | | All | |
|---|---|---|---|---|---|---|---|---|---|---|---|---|---|---|---|
| | Pre-MFA | I | II | III | G | NG | Q | NQ | S | L | D | B | M | No. | % |
| Proprietory | 9 | 10 | 12 | 15 | 31 | 15 | 35 | 11 | 20 | 26 | 28 | 13 | 5 | 46 | 26 |
| Partnership | 0 | 0 | 3 | 6 | 8 | 1 | 5 | 4 | 2 | 7 | 6 | 2 | 1 | 9 | 5 |
| Pvt. Ltd. | 13 | 16 | 8 | 11 | 39 | 9 | 44 | 4 | 40 | 8 | 42 | 3 | 3 | 48 | 27 |
| Public Ltd. | 12 | 16 | 18 | 28 | 62 | 12 | 64 | 10 | 41 | 33 | 52 | 12 | 10 | 74 | 41.8 |
| All No. | 34 | 42 | 41 | 60 | 140 | 37 | 148 | 29 | 103 | 74 | 128 | 30 | 19 | 177 | 100 |
| Firms % | 19.2 | 23.7 | 23.2 | 33.9 | 79.1 | 20.9 | 83.6 | 16.4 | 58.2 | 41.8 | 72.3 | 16.9 | 10.7 | 100 | 100 |

Note: G : Growth; Q: Quota; S: Small
NG: Non-growth; NQ: Non-quota; L: Large
D : Delhi; B: Bombay; M: Madras

Table 25

*Sales Profile of Apparel Export Firms Turnover in 1986 in Rs. 00,000*

|  | Mean | Std. Dev. | Min. | Max. | NZO's | (n) | N.R. | Z |
|---|---|---|---|---|---|---|---|---|
| REGION |  |  |  |  |  |  |  |  |
| Delhi | 123.84 | 202.55 | 1.00 | 1425.00 | 1 | 123 | 4 | 2.64 |
| Bombay | 336.71 | 400.35 | 1.50 | 1800.00 | 0 | 26 | 4 | 1.18 |
| Madras | 224.78 | 226.22 | 3.00 | 750.00 | 0 | 18 | 1 | 1.79 |
| Q/NQ Firms |  |  |  |  |  |  |  |  |
| Quota | 152.89 | 225.02 | 1.50 | 1425.00 | 1 | 140 | 7 | 1.22 |
| Non-Quota | 244.41 | 376.47 | 1.00 | 1800.00 | 0 | 27 | 2 |  |
| G/NG Firms |  |  |  |  |  |  |  |  |
| Growth | 190.92 | 280.03 | 1.00 | 1800.00 | 0 | 133 | 7 | 3.93 |
| Non-Growth | 78.99 | 88.26 | 1.50 | 325.00 | 1 | 34 | 2 |  |
| Size |  |  |  |  |  |  |  |  |
| Small | 39.48 | 26.46 | 1.00 | 100.00 | 1 | 99 | 3 | 8.15 |
| Large | 356.01 | 319.48 | 105.00 | 1800.00 | 0 | 68 | 6 ˉ |  |
| All | 167.60 | 256.22 | 1.00 | 1800.00 | 1 | 167 | 9 |  |

NZO's : No. of firms responding with a zero. (n) : No. of responding firms.
N.R. : No. of non-responding firms. Z : Z test value for difference of means.

Table 26

*Sales Profile of Apparel Export Firms, 1986 (Pcs. 00,000)*

|  | Mean | Std.Dev. | Min. | Max. | NZO's | (n) | N.R. | Z |
|---|---|---|---|---|---|---|---|---|
| REGION |  |  |  |  |  |  |  |  |
| Delhi | 2.49 | 3.71 | 0.03 | 22.00 | 1 | 114 | 13 | 3.30 |
| Bombay | 9.14 | 10.69 | 0.05 | 45.00 | 0 | 29 | 1 | 0.46 |
| Madras | 7.40 | 12.49 | 0.58 | 50.00 | 0 | 15 | 4 | 1.51 |
| Q/NQ Firms |  |  |  |  |  |  |  |  |
| Quota | 3.54 | 5.88 | 0.03 | 50.00 | 1 | 132 | 15 | 1.68 |
| Non-Quota | 7.39 | 11.41 | 0.03 | 45.00 | 0 | 26 | 3 |  |
| G/NG Firms |  |  |  |  |  |  |  |  |
| Growth | 4.54 | 7.77 | 0.03 | 50.00 | 0 | 127 | 13 | 1.90 |
| Non-Growth | 2.70 | 3.86 | 0.04 | 15.00 | 1 | 31 | 5 |  |
| Size |  |  |  |  |  |  |  |  |
| Small | 0.84 | 0.70 | 0.03 | 4.00 | 1 | 89 | 13 | 6.88 |
| Large | 8.51 | 9.24 | 0.98 | 50.00 | 0 | 69 | 5 |  |
| All | 4.17 | 7.18 | 0.03 | 50.00 | 1 | 158 | 18 |  |

NZO's : No. of firms responding with a zero. (n) : No. of responding firms.
N.R. : No. of non-responding firms. Z : Z test value for difference of means.

It appears from the foregoing that quota firms have a smaller turnover both in terms of value and quantity as compared to non-quota firms. However, this difference in turnover is significant only in case of quantum of turnover at a 10 per cent level of significance.

# 7

# Pattern of Production

Since there are only about 450 export firms in the organised manufacturing sector, a question arises as to where the bulk of the export production is undertaken. However, before this question is answered some light needs to be thrown on the production process in this industry.

There are basically three phases in the actual production process—cutting, making and finishing:

*Cutting*: The fabric is cut according to patterns by master cutters after it has been bulk-layed. In almost all cases the cutting is mechanised with the help of power-operated cutting machines.

*Making*: This involves the actual tailoring of the garment on sewing machines which is the most labour-intensive part of the production process. The sewing machines are either foot-operated or power-operated. Generally, three systems of tailoring are prevalent on the shop floor. First, individual tailoring wherein a single skilled tailor completes the whole garment. Second, production is organised on an assembly line basis. Here an individual machine operator specialises in stitching only one part of a garment. As the pieces go along an assembly line, the complete garment emerges. Third, a group of tailors (often part of an extended family, caste or village kinsmen) organise as a 'chaal'. They take a given number of pieces and divide the work among themselves in such a way that the most skilled tailor makes the difficult parts while the less skilled join the simple parts. A single person does not make the whole garment. There may be several such 'chaals' on the shop floor. A firm normally uses one of the three systems mentioned here. The assembly line system mentioned above is generally associated with power-operated machines on the Indian shop floor.

*Finishing*: Once the garment has been tailored it has to be trimmed, checked for dimensions and sent for 'finishing'. This involves washing, spot removing, ironing and packing into retail packs. The retail polybags are then packed by size and colour assortments in cardboard packages for shipment.

## COST STRUCTURE

The major part of the production time is taken by 'making' while 'cutting' and 'finishing' involve the least time and cost. A bulk of the workforce on the shop floor is employed in the sewing operations. Such labour-intensive operations have become the most difficult managerial task in Indian apparel industry today.

We can now examine the cost structure of this production process. Respondent firms were asked to indicate the relative share of cutting and making costs (fabrication costs), material costs, finishing costs and overheads. The responses are presented in Table 27 below:

**Table 27**

*Cost Structure of Apparel Production (FOB share in per cent)*

|  | Fabrication | Materials | Finishing | Overheads |
|---|---|---|---|---|
| Mean | 21.53 | 54.34 | 8.91 | 15.08 |
| (S.D.) | 6.85 | 8.84 | 4.75 | 6.38 |
| Min. | 8 | 25 | 2 | 4 |
| Max. | 50 | 80 | 30 | 39 |
| (n) | 171 | 171 | 171 | 171 |
| NR | 6 | 6 | 6 | 6 |

The highest cost component is of material costs represented by 54.3 per cent followed by fabrication costs (21.5 per cent), overheads (15 per cent) and finishing costs (8.9 per cent). The most labour-intensive operations are represented by 21.5 per cent fabrication costs. The standard deviation around this mean value is 6.85 and the range is between 8 per cent and 50 per cent on the basis of

171 firms which responded to this question. The share of fabrication cost varies depending on the value of the fabrics used in the apparel. The more expensive the fabric quality, the lower the per cent share of fabrication costs. The more complicated the style of the garment, the higher the fabrication costs. The share generally varies from style to style and 21.5 per cent share of fabrication costs is meant to represent the average for the industry. Fabrication and finishing represent direct labour costs which are about 30.4 per cent of the FOB value of apparel shipments. The remaining 15.1 per cent represents indirect cost which includes managerial overheads, depreciation and manufacturing profits. It is, however, difficult to pinpoint the share of profits due to the respondents' hesitation to provide data. A statistical analysis shows that there are no statistically significant differences in the share of labour, overheads, or material costs among different regions as well as different types of firms. Even regional variations in wage levels do not result in significant differences in contribution of labour costs to FOB value of apparel shipments.

## DECENTRALISATION

Even though the direct labour cost is only 30.4 per cent of FOB value, production remains largely a labour-intensive operation. Some 88.7 per cent of the firms have decentralised their fabrication work. They retain the cutting and finishing jobs as in-house processes and decentralise the tailoring to sub-contractors. Thousands of such sub-contractors called 'fabricators' have mushroomed in the three major centres. Located in residential, commercial and industrial areas of the metropolitan centres they serve as captive units to one or more merchant exporters. Typically a merchant-exporter obtains export orders, develops the samples, procures fabrics and materials, delivers the cut fabric and tailoring specifications to a fabricator. The exporter's staff exercise quality control at the premises of the fabrictor. The tailored garments are then finished under close supervision of the exporter. Some firms may even sub-contract the cutting and finishing operations. However, this may be rare as cutting is a cost centre that can drastically affect profits if not undertaken efficiently. Finishing is generally not sub-contracted because it affects the quality and the 'shelf-look' of this consumer product and is critical to its selling.

Sub-contractors are entrepreneurs who have specialised in tailoring operations. They can fabricate all types of garments exported from India. Investment in plant and machinery is low and they operate from low cost areas. Most of such factories attract migrant skilled and semi-skilled workers from nearby rural and semi-urban areas. When there is no work the factories are shut and workers either look for other fabricators or leave for their distant villages or homes for a forced vacation. Since work may be seasonal, the fabricators generally tend to avoid labour laws on health, insurance, provident fund, etc. Not being subject to labour laws they can close down almost immediately without any liability of terminal benefits to workers. This is not to say that workers are paid low wages. On the contrary, an average skilled worker in Delhi or Bombay may earn two or three times the legal minimum wages during the period work is available. During peak months a fabricator can double or treble his capacity by employing extra hands. As the off-season approaches he may either close down or operate with just a skeleton staff. Since the work is of uncertain continuity, most fabricators do not employ workers on a salary basis. Payments on a piece-rate system have proven to be highly productive, efficient and suited for this production environment.

Thousands of such fabricators operating in Delhi, Bombay and Madras regions have come to be the backbone of the export sector of the Indian apparel industry. Their specialised services are sought by the organised manufacturer as well. Such manufacturer-exporters engage only a minimum size of work force in their own employment. Their expansion and increasing export turnover are mainly due to their reliance on the fabricators.

A merchant-exporter may be working with two to twenty such fabricators at a time depending upon the type of garment, number of styles, shipment deadlines and export turnover. These fabricators do not occur in official statistics as manufacturing and employment units. Yet, they form the backbone of the apparel industry in India. It is true that but for this decentralised sector, Indian apparel exports would not have been where they are today. It is estimated[1] that about 79.3 per cent of the 370.1 million pieces of apparel exported from India in 1987 were produced in the decentralised sector.

[1] There were 29,503 machines installed in the organised manufacturing sector during 1987 (Rajya Sabha, unstarred question no. 3814, dated 30 August 1988). Assuming 100 per cent capacity utilisation for 300 working days in the year, the total production was 76.649 million pieces averaged at 8.66 pcs/machine per day (see Table 32). The share of the organised sector works out to only 20.7 per cent.

As many as 157 out of 175 firms who provided data with respect to reliance on decentralised production had resorted to sub-contracting and only eighteen firms reported complete in-house production. On an average, 73.6 per cent of the annual production of the firms in 1986 was done in the decentralised sector. This represented an annual average of 2,41,000 pcs per firm. A comparison of data at the terminal years of the reference period showed that reliance on decentralised production had increased to 73.6 per cent from 65.2 per cent in the initial years of the firms concerned. This difference in proportion is significant at a 10 per cent level of significance. In quantum terms this represented an increase in sub-contracted production from 86,000 pcs/firm to 2,41,000 pcs/firm in a year. This difference in the absolute quantum of sub-contracted production is significant at the 1 per cent level of significance (see Tables 28 and 29).

It has been observed that the average size of Delhi firms by turn-over in number of pieces is smaller than those in Bombay and Madras regions. These differences in turnover are significant at the 5 per cent level of significance. Despite these regional variations we observe reliance on sub-contractors by firms in each of the three regions. During the current year share of reliance of the firms on sub-contractors among Delhi firms was 79.5 per cent followed by 63.8 per cent and 48.6 per cent in Bombay and Madras regions respectively. These differences in reliance on sub-contractors between regions are significant at a 5 per cent level of significance between Delhi and Madras firms and a 1 per cent level of significance between Delhi and Bombay firms. These differences were observed even in the initial years of the firms concerned. While reliance on sub-contractors, share (per cent) in production shows no significant change in the period between the initial year and the current year of the firms concerned, yet, sub-contracted share in the number of pieces has increased from 43,000 to 2,59,000 pcs/firm in Madras and from 1,47,000 to 1,85,000 pcs/firm in Delhi regions. These differences are significant at the 1 per cent level of significance (see Tables 28 and 29).

Growth firms appear to have a larger sub-contracted turnover of 4,12,000 pcs/firm as compared to an average of 2,75,000 pcs/firm in case of non-growth firms. However, this difference is not significant even at the 10 per cent level of significance. Growth firms sub-contracted 74.11 per cent of their turnover as compared to 71.8 per cent in case of non-growth firms in the current year and this

Table 28

Decentralised Production Share (00,000 pcs.) in 1986

| | MEAN | STD.DEV. | MINIMUM | MAXIMUM | NZO's | (n) | N.R. | Z | Z' |
|---|---|---|---|---|---|---|---|---|---|
| REGION | | | | | | | | | |
| Delhi | 1.85 | 3.06 | 0.00 | 22.00 | 12.00 | 120.00 | 8.00 | 2.32 | 3.43 |
| Bombay | 4.65 | 6.31 | 0.00 | 32.00 | 3.00 | 29.00 | 1.00 | 1.49 | 2.60 |
| Madras | 2.59 | 2.97 | 0.00 | 7.50 | 3.00 | 16.00 | 3.00 | 0.93 | 2.84 |
| Q/NQ Firms | | | | | | | | | |
| Quota | 2.25 | 3.32 | 0.00 | 22.00 | 16.00 | 138.00 | 10.00 | 0.82 | 4.79 |
| Non-Quota | 3.26 | 6.24 | 0.00 | 32.00 | 2.00 | 27.00 | 2.00 | | 1.50 |
| G/NG Firms | | | | | | | | | |
| Growth | 2.57 | 4.22 | 0.00 | 32.00 | 13.00 | 131.00 | 9.00 | 1.31 | 4.73 |
| Non-Growth | 1.81 | 2.60 | 0.00 | 10.00 | 5.00 | 34.00 | 3.00 | | 0.83 |
| Size | | | | | | | | | |
| Small | 0.63 | 0.69 | 0.00 | 4.00 | 14.00 | 95.00 | 8.00 | 6.84 | 2.25 |
| Large | 4.83 | 5.10 | 0.00 | 32.00 | 4.00 | 70.00 | 4.00 | | 5.03 |
| All | 2.41 | 3.94 | 0.00 | 32.00 | 18.00 | 165.00 | 12.00 | | 4.68 |

NZO's : No. of firms responding with a zero.
(n) : No. of responding firms.
N.R. : No. of non-responding firms.
Z : Z test value for difference of means.
Z' : Z test value for difference of means in 1986 and initial year.

TABLE 29

*Decentralised Production Share (00,000 pcs.) in Initial Year*

| | MEAN | STD.DEV. | MINIMUM | MAXIMUM | NZO's | (n) | N.R. | Z |
|---|---|---|---|---|---|---|---|---|
| *REGION* | | | | | | | | |
| Delhi | 0.77 | 1.54 | 0.00 | 11.40 | 22.00 | 111.00 | 17.00 | 1.87 |
| Bombay | 1.47 | 1.85 | 0.00 | 6.30 | 7.00 | 29.00 | 1.00 | 2.74 |
| Madras | 0.43 | 0.66 | 0.00 | 2.50 | 7.00 | 17.00 | 2.00 | 1.57 |
| *Q/NQ Firms* | | | | | | | | |
| Quota | 0.76 | 1.50 | 0.00 | 11.40 | 32.00 | 132.00 | 16.00 | 1.64 |
| Non-Quota | 1.38 | 1.77 | 0.00 | 6.00 | 4.00 | 25.00 | 4.00 | |
| *G/NG Firms* | | | | | | | | |
| Growth | 0.75 | 1.24 | 0.00 | 6.30 | 25.00 | 126.00 | 14.00 | 1.19 |
| Non-Growth | 1.29 | 2.44 | 0.00 | 11.40 | 11.00 | 31.00 | 6.00 | |
| *Size* | | | | | | | | |
| Small | 0.39 | 0.76 | 0.00 | 6.04 | 20.00 | 91.00 | 12.00 | 4.20 |
| Large | 1.51 | 2.07 | 0.00 | 11.40 | 16.00 | 66.00 | 8.00 | |
| *All* | 0.86 | 1.56 | 0.00 | 11.40 | 36.00 | 157.00 | 20.008 | |

NZO's : No. of firms responding with a zero.
(n) : No. of responding firms.
N.R. : No. of non-responding firms.
Z : Z test value for difference of means.

difference is not significant. These firms had a somewhat larger level of reliance on sub-contractors during their initial years, yet these inter-firm differences were not significant both in terms of proportion as well as number of pieces of sub-contracted production. We can observe that growth firms have increased their reliance on sub-contractors much more than non-growth firms during the period under reference in number of pieces. Reliance on sub-contracting increased from 75,000 to 2,57,000 pcs/firm in case of growth firms and from 1,29,000 to 1,81,000 pcs/firm in case of non-growth firms over the reference period. While this change is significant (at a 1 per cent level of significance) in case of growth firms, it does not appear so in case of non-growth firms. An inference that can be drawn here is that the firm's ability to sub-contract its production is vital for its growth. A firm that shows resilience appears to have a higher affinity for growth in this industry. What is important is not the actual share of decentralised production, but the change in number of pieces sub-contracted over the reference period.

Quota and non-quota firms also appear to have no significant difference in per cent share of decentralised production both in their initial and current years. Yet, it can be observed that quota firms have enhanced their reliance on sub-contracting from 63.1 per cent to 73.1 per cent over the reference period and this difference is significant at the 10 per cent level of significance. There is no such difference in case of non-quota firms. Quota firms have also increased their sub-contracted turnover from 76,000 to 2,25,000 pcs/firm as compared to the change of 1,38,000 to 3,26,000 pcs/firm in case of non-quota firms. The difference is significant at a 1 per cent level of significance in case of quota firms as compared to change in non-quota firms. This shows that there has been a larger shift to the decentralised sector among quota firms as compared to non-quota firms over this period.

One of the reasons this happens is because of the uncertainty generated in the micro-environment of the firm under the present quota regime. In the first phase sample, 88.5 per cent of quota firms confirmed that the quota system created uncertainty in their business (sixty-three out of sixty-nine firms). Since by definition, non-quota firms also exported 39 per cent or less of quota items they also faced such uncertainty insofar as their export of quota items was concerned (see Table 30). A firm which exports only non-quota items would be free of the uncertainty created by quotas. Responding

Table 30

*Managerial Uncertainty in Business: No. of Responses*

|  | Quota firms | Non-quota firms | All Firms |
|---|---|---|---|
| Yes | 63 | 12 | 75 |
| No | 6 | 4 | 10 |
| (n) | 69 | 16 | 85 |
| *Areas of uncertainty* | | | |
| a Production Planning | 48 | 8 | 56 |
| b Marketing | 51 | 9 | 60 |
| c Financial Management | 26 | 2 | 28 |
| d Investment in New Machinery | 10 | 1 | 11 |
| e Expansion diversification | 24 | 3 | 27 |
| f Any other | 5 | 3 | 8 |

**Source:** Q11 Questionnaire Phase I.

firms were asked to state the specific decision areas affected by such uncertainty. An analysis of the response in Table 30 shows that marketing and production planning were the most seriously affected areas. The other areas affected were financial management and expansion/diversification of the business. Apart from the adverse effect this uncertainty generates upon management, it motivates the firm to reduce its fixed costs to hedge risks. Future availability of quotas to the firm are dependent on a number of variables beyond the firm's control, hence there is a tendency for retaining only a minimum viable scale of in-house production. Vital production functions like quality control, product research and development, cutting, designing, and finishing are centralised while fabrication is decentralised to the maximum extent possible. This decentralised share is as high as 73.63 per cent in our sample. In most cases the centralised share of fabrication is the capacity for which the firm is assured of quotas as well as lean period orders. It can safely be inferred that the greater tendency among quota firms to decentralise production is influenced by the climate of uncertainty created under the quota regime.

We can now analyse the reasons given by firms for resorting to decentralised production. As shown by Table 31 of the most frequently occurring reason for such decentralisation was 'avoid labour problems', followed by 'easier to manage', 'to overcome seasonal fluctuations' and 'to overcome shipment deadlines'. This was true

Table 31

Reasons for Decentralisation: Number of Firms

| Reasons | Delhi | | Bombay | | Madras | | Small | | Large | | All | Quota | | Non-Quota | |
|---|---|---|---|---|---|---|---|---|---|---|---|---|---|---|---|
| | n | n.r. | n | n.r. | n | n.r. | n | n.r. | n | n.r. | | n | n.r. | n | n.r. |
| (a) | 20 | 1 | 6 | 2 | 6 | 5 | 17 | 4 | 15 | 4 | 32 | 25 | 8 | 7 | 0 |
| (b) | 33 | 1 | 21 | 2 | 7 | 5 | 25 | 4 | 36 | 4 | 61 | 48 | 8 | 13 | 0 |
| (c) | 13 | 1 | 3 | 2 | 6 | 5 | 8 | 4 | 14 | 4 | 22 | 16 | 8 | 6 | 0 |
| (d) | 14 | 1 | 6 | 2 | 9 | 5 | 8 | 4 | 21 | 4 | 29 | 26 | 8 | 3 | 0 |
| (e) | 15 | 1 | 8 | 2 | 4 | 5 | 12 | 4 | 15 | 4 | 27 | 25 | 8 | 2 | 0 |
| (f) | 15 | 1 | 2 | 2 | 4 | 5 | 9 | 4 | 12 | 4 | 21 | 18 | 8 | 3 | 0 |
| (g) | 2 | 1 | 3 | 2 | 3 | 5 | 3 | 4 | 5 | 4 | 8 | 6 | 8 | 2 | 0 |

Source : Q5 (d) Questionnaire Phase I.
Note  : (a)–Easier to Manage
       (b)–Avoid labour problems
       (c)–More Economical
       (d)–To overcome seasonal fluctuations
       (e)–To overcome shipment deadlines
       (f)–To overcome problems caused by laws
       (g)–Any other
n  : number of firms responding
nr  : non-responding firms

for small and large firms as well. There were no major differences on the reasons for decentralisation between quota and non-quota firms. A similar situation prevailed in all the three geographical centres.

It is apparent that quotas alone could not have caused increasing reliance on decentralisation. The labour-intensive fabrication function involves labour problems that require constant and careful managerial attention. The export firm sought to reduce executive time spent on labour problems by decentralising production. Managers found such a system 'easier to manage', as they could devote their attention to other managerial tasks. Since export demand was of a seasonal nature, they could not afford to employ full time permanent workers. Such workers would have little work during off-season and overall labour costs would rise. Also since export orders were to be shipped within short lead times, often large-sized orders had to be sub-contracted to meet the deadlines. There were manufacturer-exporters in the organised sector, but they were few. Tables 28 and 29 show that in their initial years thirty-six firms did not use sub-contractors at all. By 1986 half of these firms had shifted production to sub-contractors substantially. Of these firms sixteen were quota firms and only two were non-quota firms. Labour and social security laws tended to be a disincentive and most firms associated centralised production with higher overheads and legal surveillance. Many firms registered with the AEPC as manufacturers are not recognised as such by the official Textile Commissioner. The Textile Commissioner's office insists on social security laws relating to provident fund and employee state insurance for workers. Most firms are unable to meet these requirements as local authorities and state governments have conflicting rules and half-yearly reporting statements required by the Textile Commissioner are hard to come by. Some firms indicated that these could be obtained for a price but the costs of getting them sometimes outweighed the benefits of such registration. Larger factories were more prone to unionisation and labour trouble which the firms wanted to avoid at all costs, particularly in Bombay and Delhi. At the firm level there appeared to be good reasons for increased reliance on decentralised production to overcome diseconomies of centralisation.

We can now state our findings in regard to Hypothesis 5, viz., *'Under a quota regime export firms generally tend to decentralise production operations due to diseconomies of centralisation'*. Hypothesis 5 is found to be proven on the premise that export firms have decentralised their production operations due to diseconomies associated with centralisation as explained in the foregoing pages. However, this should not be taken to mean that the quota regime is the sole cause for this. Quite a few factors analysed previously have contributed to the emergence of decentralised patterns of production. The quota regime has accentuated the impact of these domestic factors on decentralisation.

## PRODUCTIVITY

Two distinct production systems co-exist in this industry. One using manually-operated machines and the other using power-operated machines. Respondent firms provided data in average number of apparel pieces produced per machine per day for five major types of apparel. The data for both types of production systems are easily comparable. Table 32 shows the differences in productivity among the two production systems by size as well as region. The sample in this study shows significant differences in productivity among the manual-and power-operated systems. These differences are significant for all five items (at the 5 per cent level of significance in respect of blouses and at a 1 per cent level for all other items). Productivity gains are highly significant (at a 1 per cent level ) among small firms for each of the five items. Among large firms differences are not at all significant for blouses and shirts, while they are highly significant for trousers (at a 1 per cent level), and significant for dresses and skirts at 5 per cent and 10 per cent levels of significance respectively.

Table 32

*Productivity on Manual and Power Machines:*
*Average Number of pieces per Machine/Day*

| Items | National | | Delhi | | Bombay | | Madras | | Small | | Large | |
|---|---|---|---|---|---|---|---|---|---|---|---|---|
| | M | P | M | P | M | P | M | P | M | P | M | P |
| Blouses | 9.4 | 12.7** | 9.3 | 12.3** | 10.1 | 16.0 | 8.5 | 8.7 | 9.0 | 10.9*** | 9.8 | 14.4 |
| Dresses | 5.6 | 7.2*** | 5.6 | 7.5*** | 5.9 | 7.1 | 6.0 | 6.3 | 5.7 | 7.6*** | 5.5 | 6.8** |
| Shirts | 8.2 | 10.3*** | 8.0 | 11.3*** | 9.1 | 10.3 | 8.4 | 7.9 | 8.2 | 11.2*** | 8.3 | 9.7* |
| Skirts | 8.2 | 11.2*** | 8.2 | 11.2*** | 7.4 | 12.9 | 9.0 | 8.8 | 8.3 | 10.8*** | 7.9 | 11.7* |
| Trousers | 6.0 | 7.8*** | 6.0 | 7.8*** | 6.7 | 8.9* | 5.2 | 6.0 | 6.2 | 7.8*** | 5.9 | 7.8*** |

Note: ***, **, * is significant at 1%, 5%, 10% level of significance respectively.
     M: manual; P: power

Among the regions there are no significant differences for all five items among firms in Madras and for four items among Bombay firms. Among Delhi firms these differences are highly significant at a 1 per cent level of significance for four items and significant (at the 5 per cent level) for blouses. These comparisons show that power-operated production systems offer significant gains in productivity for important segments of the industry. Insignificant gains in other segments of the industry can be attributed to variations in skill levels and work flow methods.

Apart from productivity differences among the two production systems, there are also differences in productivity using the same system among certain segments of the industry. Productivity among

Delhi firms using power machines is significantly higher than Madras and Bombay firms for skirts (at the 1 per cent and 10 per cent levels respectively) and for blouses (at the 5 per cent level) produced in Madras. Productivity for trousers made on power machines is significantly lower in Madras as compared to Bombay ( at a 1 per cent level) and Delhi (at the 5 per cent level). There appear to be no significant differences in productivity levels among different types of firms using manual machines.

A point can be made here in regard to productivity differences among the growth and non-growth firms using power machines. Productivity levels are significantly higher among growth firms in production of dresses (at a 1 per cent level), blouses, skirts and trousers (at the 5 per cent level). This could be one of the reasons for lack of competitiveness among non-growth firms.

Another notable point is that there are no significant differences in productivity between large and small firms in any type of production systems. It can be inferred that economies of scale in production do not enhance productivity in any significant manner in this industry.

This inference is supported by the Z-value for difference of mean daily production per machine among small and large firms which varies between .09 and 1.16. This difference is insignificant for all five items in manual as well as power-operated systems.

## COST SAVINGS

We have so far observed that there are significant productivity gains in using power-operated machines in certain segments of the industry. Table 33 shows the cost savings per piece of apparel in segments where productivity differences are significant. These savings vary between Re. 0.61 to Re. 0.98 per piece for the industry as a whole. It will be seen that these savings reflect a very small share (1.1 to 1.8 per cent) of the Rs. 55.07 average FOB price of apparel shipments of the firms concerned (see Table 34). Whatever savings that occur in using power machines are offset by costs associated with mechanisation. We can point out the following four types of costs that appear to neutralise the cost savings mentioned here.

### Training Costs

A large bulk of apparel workers are not very familiar with power-

### Table 33

#### Labour Cost Savings Using Power Machines (per piece)

| Items | | National | Delhi | Bombay | Small Firms | Large Firms |
|---|---|---|---|---|---|---|
| Blouses: | Rs. | 0.68 | 0.77 | – | 0.50 | – |
| | ($) | (0.05) | (0.06) | – | (0.04) | – |
| Dresses: | Rs. | 0.98 | 1.34 | – | 1.14 | 0.83 |
| | ($) | (0.08) | (0:10) | – | (0.09) | 0.06 |
| Shirts: | Rs. | 0.61 | 1.07 | – | 0.86 | – |
| | ($) | (0.05) | (0.08) | – | (0.07) | – |
| Skirts: | Rs. | 0.80 | 0.96 | – | 0.73 | 0.98 |
| | ($) | (0.06) | (0.07) | – | (0.06) | (0.08) |
| Trousers: | Rs. | 0.94 | 1.13 | 0.97 | 0.86 | 0.97 |
| | ($) | (0.07) | (0.09) | (0.07) | (0.07) | (0.08) |
| Daily | Rs. | 24.40 | 29.47 | 26.36 | 26.05 | 23.68 |
| Wages | ($) | (1.88) | (2.27) | (2.03) | (2.01) | (1.83) |

**Note:** US $: Rs. 12.962 during 1987. Wages for floor shop workers based on 26 days month.

### Table 34

#### Average Price Per Piece in 1986 (Rs.)

| | Mean | Std. Dev. | Minimum | Maximum | NZO's | (n) | N.R. | Z |
|---|---|---|---|---|---|---|---|---|
| *REGION* | | | | | | | | |
| Delhi | 56.66 | 30.26 | 10.00 | 275.00 | 1 | 121 | 6 | 0.51 |
| Bombay | 53.86 | 23.57 | 15.00 | 100.00 | 0 | 25 | 5 | 1.49 |
| Madras | 44.16 | 17.29 | 12.00 | 80.00 | 0 | 15 | 4 | 2.39 |
| *Q/NQ Firms* | | | | | | | | |
| Quota | 53.18 | 18.60 | 12.00 | 106.67 | 1 | 135 | 12 | 1.04 |
| Non-Quota | 64.92 | 56.83 | 10.00 | 275.00 | 0 | 26 | 3 | |
| *G/NG Firms* | | | | | | | | |
| Growth | 56.27 | 30.07 | 10.00 | 275.00 | 0 | 129 | 11 | 1.32 |
| Non-Growth | 50.35 | 20.74 | 13.00 | 100.00 | 1 | 32 | 4 | |
| *Size* | | | | | | | | |
| Small | 55.45 | 32.39 | 10.00 | 275.00 | 1 | 96 | 6 | 0.23 |
| Large | 54.49 | 21.53 | 12.00 | 106.67 | 0 | 65 | 9 | |
| *All* | 55.07 | 28.46 | 10.00 | 275.00 | 1 | 161 | 15 | |

NZO's: No. of firms responding with a zero.
(n)   : No. of responding firms.
N.R.  : No. of non-responding firms.
Z     : Z test value for difference of means.

operated machines. There are hardly any training institutions where such skills can be learnt. So employers have to train workers on the job and this involves costs.

## Unionisation Costs

Mechanisation also requires employment of permanent skilled workers. Employers in this industry are wary of employing a large permanent workforce which can easily unionise. Unionisation has proven extremely risky in this industry where export shipments have deadlines and late shipments usually become dead-stock with no buyers. There is another disincentive in employing a permanent workforce due to the seasonal nature of the demand. Lay-offs are very difficult to manage if the workforce is unionised.

## Higher Overheads

Power-operated machines require a higher investment as well as a larger expense on repair, maintainance and breakdown costs. Power machine operators expect higher wages as compared to manual machine operators. An employer can anticipate the impact of future wage increases relative to the gains in productivity.

## Other Costs

Power breakdowns occur frequently and without notice. Losses from work stoppage due to loadshedding can be substantial. Another factor is the lack of managerial experience in organising assembly line type of workflow methods generally associated with power machines. Increases in productivity are also dependent on length of production runs per style, the workflow methods and idle time considerations. Sometimes, the type of fabric also influences productivity: for example, the productivity in manufacture of matched and balanced checks/stripes apparel is lower as compared to other type of fabrics.

The foregoing analysis explains the slow diffusion of mechanised production systems in the Indian apparel industry. A very small number of firms are using power-operated production systems while manual-operating systems dominate the industry. There are clear gains in quality with power-operated machines. Firms which are mechanised have been influenced more by quality considerations rather than cost savings through increase in labour productivity. Power machines give better and uniform stitching resulting in better shelf-look to a garment. Workers do not tire quickly on power machines and can work longer hours.

## EMPLOYMENT

We now go on to examine the Hypothesis 7, viz., '*Quotas have adversely affected the employment in the Indian Apparel Industry*'. Before this is done we will analyse the employment levels and wage rates prevailing in the industry.

Even though a large share of production is decentralised by the firm, yet it has a core of full-time employees. The average number of employees per firm is 177.25. However there is a very wide standard deviation of 347 around this mean as the number of workers varies between one and 5,000. Table 35 shows that small firms employ an average of 46.6 workers as compared to 349 workers in large firms. Employment in non-quota firms tends to be more than twice as large when compared to quota firms. Non-growth firms on the other hand are having smaller employment than growth firms.

Employment data in Table 35 show that firms in the Bombay region have the highest employment of 493.3 workers per firm followed by 359.4 and 71.9 workers per firm in the Madras and Delhi regions respectively. This indicates that direct employment per firm in the Delhi region is quite small as compared to the firms in Bombay and Madras and their difference is significant at the 5 and 1 per cent levels respectively. The average Bombay and Madras firms employ more workers than the average Delhi firm.

The monthly wage bill of the average firm is about Rs. 1,20,000 per month. This works out to an average salary of Rs. 677 per month. Sample data show that there are wide regional variations in wage rates. The Delhi apparel worker earns Rs. 1156.1 per month which is 2.3 times the wages in Bombay (Rs. 504.8 per month) and 2.5 times the wages in Madras (Rs. 456.3 per month). Another important factor revealed is that workers in small firms earn Rs. 815.6

Table 35

*Employment Profile of Firms : Total No. of Staff*

|  | *Mean* | *Std. Dev.* | *Minimum* | *Maximum* | *NZO's* | *(n)* | *N.R.* | *Z* |
|---|---|---|---|---|---|---|---|---|
| *REGION* | | | | | | | | |
| Delhi | 71.79 | 114.04 | 1.00 | 850.00 | 2.00 | 121.00 | 5.00 | 2.17 |
| Bombay | 493.30 | 1064.30 | 1.00 | 5000.00 | 0.00 | 30.00 | 0.00 | 0.61 |
| Madras | 359.44 | 418.63 | 50.00 | 1800.00 | 1.00 | 18.00 | 0.00 | 2.90 |
| *Q/NQ Firms* | | | | | | | | |
| Quota | 148.55 | 459.12 | 1.00 | 5000.00 | 2.00 | 142.00 | 4.00 | 1.32 |
| Non-Quota | 328.19 | 675.82 | 3.00 | 2800.00 | 1.00 | 27.00 | 1.00 | |
| *G/NG Firms* | | | | | | | | |
| Growth | 202.17 | 560.34 | 2.00 | 5000.00 | 2.00 | 133.00 | 5.00 | 2.23 |
| Non-Growth. | 85.19 | 119.09 | 1.00 | 582.00 | 1.00 | 36.00 | 0.00 | |
| *Size* | | | | | | | | |
| Small | 46.59 | 71.33 | 1.00 | 458.00 | 2.00 | 96.00 | 5.00 | 3.54 |
| Large | 349.07 | 726.98 | 9.00 | 5000.00 | 1.00 | 73.00 | 0.00 | |
| *All* | 177.25 | 501.95 | 1.00 | 5000.00 | 3.00 | 169.00 | 5.00 | |

NZO's : No. of firms responding with a zero.
(n)    : No. of responding firms.
N.R.   : No. of non-responding firms.
Z      : Z test value for difference of means.

per month which is 21.7 per cent higher than the earnings of the average worker (Rs. 670.3 per month) in large firms. This datum explodes the myth that workers in smaller firms generally earn less than their counterparts in larger firms.

Workers in non-growth firms earn about Rs. 208.93 more per month as compared to their counterparts in growth firms. Non-growth firms have not been able to increase their turnover during the reference period. Higher labour costs would adversely affect the cost competitiveness of the non-growth firms. The inability of such firms to keep their labour costs under control can be partly the cause of their low competitiveness reflected in stagnating sales. We also notice that wages of workers in non-quota firms (Rs. 723.6 per month) are 11.7 per cent higher than workers in quota firms (Rs. 648.5 per month). However, no inference can be drawn from this variation.

Despite the labour-cost differentials by size, region or type of firm the average Indian hourly wage rate works out to US $ 0.25[2] for·

[2] Computed from sample data US $ : Rs. 12.962. On the basis of Rs. 677 per worker per month for 26-day month and 8-hour day.

1986–87. In spring 1987, according to Werner International Data, hourly wage rates in Hong Kong, Taiwan and South Korea were US $ 1.93, 2.09, and 1.77 respectively. However, labour productivity levels of Indian firms are considered to be as low as 20 to 25 per cent of those prevailing in the Big-3 apparel exporting countries of the Far East. Indian productivity being low, the comparative advantage to India has in terms of low wage rates is significantly eroded. However, rising wages in the Big-3 suppliers are putting Indian firms at an advantage. The nature of this advantage is however uncertain in the absence of meaningful international comparisons of hourly wage rates and productivity of apparel workers.

The apparel exporting firms employ a wide variety of workers who can be broadly classified in two categories:

1. *Managerial and Supervisory Personnel.* This category includes managers, designers, master cutters, production supervisors, and other professionals including office and commercial staff. Among the 164 firms that provided disaggregated data, the average employment in this category was 24.91 workers per firm accounting for a monthly wage bill of Rs. 47,000. This works out to an average salary of Rs. 1883 per month (US $ 145.3) for a worker in this category. On an average 1.4 out of ten workers in a firm belonged to this category.

2. *Tailors and other Shop floor Staff.* This category includes mainly blue collar shop floor workers who operate different types of machines. The largest number among this category are generally tailoring machine operators. It also includes helpers, assistants, finishing workers, washermen, etc. On the average a firm employing 155 such workers accounts for a monthly wage bill of Rs. 95,000. This works out to an average monthly earning of Rs. 613.9 per worker (US $ 47.3). Out of ten apparel workers 8.8 belong to this category.

## EMPLOYMENT LOSS

Apparel firms in the first phase sample were asked about employment loss resulting from non-availability of quotas. The responses are presented in Table 36. Only 26.5 per cent firms (twenty-two of eighty-three) reported employment loss of such type. Of these, twenty firms were quota firms and only two firms were non-quota firms. The loss relates to direct employment in the reporting firms and does not cover loss of employment in the decentralised

sector. On the basis of data provided by reporting firms, it was estimated that a total of 14,609 man-months were lost in a flexible
reference period of twelve months during MFA-III. This represents
a loss of 768.92 man-months per firm (see Table 37). The loss was
negligible among two non-quota firms—only 65 man-months per
firm. In case of quota firms the loss was as much as 851.73
man-months per firm.

Table 36

*Employment Loss Reported: No. of Firms*

|         | Quota | Non-Quota | All |
|---------|-------|-----------|-----|
| Loss    | 20    | 2         | 22  |
| No loss | 47    | 14        | 61  |
| (n)     | 67    | 16        | 83  |
| n.r.    | 2     | 2         | 2   |

Source: Q 10 of Questionnaire Phase I.
Note   : n: total number of firms.
          nr: non-responding firms.

Table 37

*Man Months Lost per Firm*

|        | Quota  | Non-Quota | All    |
|--------|--------|-----------|--------|
| Mean   | 851.73 | 65        | 768.92 |
| Min.   | 12.5   | 40        | 12.5   |
| Max.   | 7200   | 90        | 7200   |
| (N)    | 17     | 2         | 19     |
| N.R.   | 52     | 14        | 66     |

Source: Q 10 of Questionnaire Phase I.

Except for five firms all other firms reported seasonal retrenchment during two-off seasons—namely, April to July and July to
September. Discussion outside the structured frame revealed that in
many of these cases the loss in employment was more related to
off-season low demand than non-availability of quota. In some of
these cases labour trouble and unionisation had aggravated the
problem caused by quotas. Many firms hesitated to retrench workers
if work stoppage was of a temporary nature as they did not want to
lose trained workers. There were several cases where retrenchment
was partly caused by non-availability of quotas. The reported loss
in employment cannot be directly attributed only to the quota

regime. Hence, Hypothesis 7 is not proven. However, since our sample has not covered fabricators in the decentralised sector, these results do not reflect the loss of employment (if any) suffered by them. Since as much as 73.6 per cent of the production was undertaken in this sector loss of employment in this sector is bound to exist. However, no estimates are possible without reliable data on this sector. It is for the AEPC besides the Textile Commissioner,Government of India, to collect and maintain reliable statistics on this sector. In the absence of such data nothing more can be said on this point in the present study.

## INVESTMENT

The low capital intensity of the apparel industry is revealed by Table 39 which shows that the investment in plant and machinery is only an average of Rs. 8,94,000 per firm. There is very wide deviation as the range of such investment varies between Rs. 2,000 and Rs. 30 million. Barring a very few, almost all firms would be described as small-scale industry using the classification norms of the Government of India. Twenty-four firms have no investment in plant and machinery. This indicates a total reliance on the decentralised sector for production. There are significant differences (at a 1 per cent level) in investment between small and large firms. Table 39 also shows that the average investment for a small firm is Rs. 1,76,000 which represents about 40.7 machines per firm. The average investment is Rs. 1.77 million for large firms which represents about 251.3 machines per firm (Tables 38 and 39). The average investment per machine works out to Rs. 7,062 in case of large firms and Rs. 4,320 in case of small firms. This is not to say that small firms use only manual machines and large firms only power machines. Even small firms use power machines in cutting, embroidery, buttoning, overlock and some other operations in combination with manually-operated tailoring machines. Larger firms use mechanisation in finishing as well as tailoring operations. On the whole it can be stated that larger firms have a higher per machine capital investment due to use of a larger share of power-operated machines than small firms as revealed by Tables 38 and 39. Going by the sample data the labour: capital ratio works out to 19.8 workers per 1,00,000 rupees of capital investment. This is equivalent to 257 workers per US

### Table 38

#### Total No. of Machines

| | Mean | Std. Dev. | Minimum | Maximum | NZO's | (n) | N.R. | Z |
|---|---|---|---|---|---|---|---|---|
| REGION | | | | | | | | |
| Delhi | 79.13 | 274.97 | 1.00 | 2700.00 | 21.00 | 100.00 | 7.00 | 2.08 |
| Bombay | 331.00 | 622.46 | 4.00 | 2333.00 | 2.00 | 28.00 | 0.00 | 1.30 |
| Madras | 171.50 | 144.52 | 43.00 | 580.00 | 1.00 | 18.00 | 0.00 | 2.11 |
| Q/NQ Firms | | | | | | | | |
| Quota | 116.28 | 328.23 | 1.00 | 2700.00 | 19.00 | 123.00 | 6.00 | 1.25 |
| Non-Quota | 259.39 | 529.63 | 2.00 | 2333.00 | 5.00 | 23.00 | 1.00 | |
| G/NG Firms | | | | | | | | |
| Growth | 149.81 | 401.70 | 1.00 | 2700.00 | 17.00 | 118.00 | 5.00 | 1.18 |
| Non-Growth | 92.50 | 167.49 | 2.00 | 900.00 | 7.00 | 28.00 | 2.00 | |
| Size | | | | | | | | |
| Small | 40.74 | 51.61 | 1.00 | 320.00 | 18.00 | 78.00 | 7.00 | 3.35 |
| Large | 251.32 | 516.81 | 2.00 | 2700.00 | 6.00 | 68.00 | 0.00 | |
| All | 138.82 | 368.70 | 1.00 | 2700.00 | 24.00 | 146.00 | 7.00 | |

NZO's : No. of firms responding with a zero.
(n)  : No. of responding firms.
N.R.  : No. of non-responding firms.
Z  : Z test value for difference of means.

### Table 39

#### Total Value of Installed Machines (Rs. 00,000)

| | Mean | Std. Dev. | Minimum | Maximum | NZO's | (n) | N.R. | Z |
|---|---|---|---|---|---|---|---|---|
| REGION | | | | | | | | |
| Delhi | 4.23 | 14.42 | 0.02 | 140.00 | 21.00 | 99.00 | 8.00 | 1.68 |
| Bombay | 27.63 | 66.28 | 0.06 | 300.00 | 2.00 | 23.00 | 5.00 | 1.16 |
| Madras | 11.25 | 10.65 | 1.21 | 40.00 | 1.00 | 16.00 | 2.00 | 2.32 |
| Q/NQ Firms | | | | | | | | |
| Quota | 6.78 | 28.04 | 0.02 | 300.00 | 19.00 | 117.00 | 12.00 | 1.52 |
| Non-Quota | 21.01 | 41.35 | 0.03 | 140.00 | 5.00 | 21.00 | 3.00 | |
| G/NG Firms | | | | | | | | |
| Growth | 9.34 | 33.26 | 0.02 | 300.00 | 17.00 | 113.00 | 10.00 | 0.52 |
| Non-Growth | 7.13 | 14.52 | 0.03 | 70.00 | 7.00 | 25.00 | 5.00 | |
| Size | | | | | | | | |
| Small | 1.76 | 2.11 | 0.02 | 8.72 | 18.00 | 76.00 | 9.00 | 2.84 |
| Large | 17.75 | 44.35 | 0.01 | 300.00 | 6.00 | 62.00 | 6.00 | |
| All | 8.94 | 30.69 | 0.02 | 300.00 | 24.00 | 138.00 | 15.00 | |

NZO's : No. of firms responding with a zero.
(n)  : No. of responding firms.
N.R.  : No. of non-responding firms.
Z  : Z test value for difference of means.

$ 100,000 of capital investment. Among small firms this ratio is 26.5 as compared to 19.7 workers per Rs. 100,000 of capital invest ment among large apparel firms. The machine-man ratio in the industry is 1:1.28 and there are no major differences in this ratio among large and small firms. For small firms the machine-man ratio is 1:1.14 and for large firms it is 1:1.39. This only shows that the industry has very low capital intensity. The investment per employee works out to Rs. 5,043.7 which is a meagre US $389 per employee[3]. This is believed to be among the lowest in the world apparel industry.

To examine the impact of the quota regime on investment in this industry, respondents in the first phase sample were asked about their capacity expansion during the period of MFA-III. The responses in Table 40 show that 41 per cent (thirty-five firms) respondents had expanded their capacity at one time or other during MFA-III. Only four of them were non-quota firms while the rest were quota firms. This shows that a substantial number of quota firms had expanded their capacity during the reference period. The average number of new machines installed by thirty-one quota firms was 90.8 as com-pared to 82.48 in case of non-quota firms. This showed that a large segment of the quota firms were not inhibited to add capacity even during the MFA-III.

The firms also provided data on their future plans for capacity expansion. Some 63 per cent of the firms reported that they planned to increase their capacity in the near future. Among quota firms 65 per cent respondents were also ready to increase capacity in the future, i.e., during MFA-IV (see Table 41). Asked about their planned modes of such capacity expansion, it was found that among fifty-two firms proposing expansion, sixteen firms (31 per cent) favoured expansion of their capacity by increased reliance on fabri-cators in the decentralised sector (Table 42). Around 33 per cent firms wanted to install power-operated machines while 19 per cent favoured a combination of using new power machines as well as relying on fabricators. The expansion strategy favoured was either use of more power machines or increased reliance on fabricators or both. The climate of uncertainty generated by the quota regime motivated firms to use fabricators as much as they could.

From the foregoing it appears that the quota regime has not adversely affected growth of real investment in the industry. However,

[3] US $ = Rs. 12.962 being average exchange rate in 1987.

### Table 40

#### Reported Expansion in Capacity (1982–85)

|       | Quota | Non-quota | All |
|-------|-------|-----------|-----|
| Yes   | 31    | 4         | 35  |
| No    | 36    | 12        | 48  |
| (n)   | 67    | 16        | 83  |
| N.R.  | 2     | 0         | 2   |

**Source:** Q 16A of Questionnaire Phase I.

### Table 41

#### Proposed Expansion in Capacity: No. of Firms

|       | Quota | Non-quota | All |
|-------|-------|-----------|-----|
| Yes   | 45    | 7         | 52  |
| No    | 22    | 9         | 31  |
| (n)   | 67    | 16        | 83  |
| N.R.  | 2     | 0         | 2   |

**Source:** Q 16B Questionnaire Phase I.

### Table 42

#### Modes of Proposed Expansion: No. of Firms

|   |                       | Quota | Non-quota | All |
|---|-----------------------|-------|-----------|-----|
| a | More Manual Machines  | 3     | 1         | 4   |
| b | More Power Machines   | 15    | 2         | 17  |
| c | More Fabricators      | 15    | 1         | 16  |
| a & c |                   | 4     | 0         | 4   |
| a & b |                   | 0     | 1         | 1   |
| b & c |                   | 8     | 2         | 10  |
| (n)   |                   | 45    | 7         | 52  |
| N.R.  |                   | 24    | 9         | 33  |

**Source:** Q 16B Questionnaire Phase I.

this climate has also created a situation whereby 52 per cent of quota firms had not expanded capacity during MFA-III and 32 per cent of quota firms had no plans for future. A worsening of the situation during MFA-IV would affect these plans adversely. In the overall analysis it could not be proven that the quota regime had adversely affected the growth of real investment in the whole industry. Hence Hypothesis 8 *'Quotas have adversely affected growth of real investment in the Indian apparel industry'* was not proven.

## FOREIGN PRODUCTION

Out of the 177 firms twenty-three covered in the survey attempted a strategy of foreign production in order to overcome the adverse impact of binding quotas. The production for export orders was shifted to neighbouring countries where quotas had not become binding. This was mainly attempted by firms having bulk orders from the USA during 1983 to 1987. In almost all cases a local manufacturing facility was located. Indian fabrics and tailoring materials approved by the importer were exported to the neighbouring country. Technical assistance in the form of supervisory production personnel were also sent to supervise the production process. The finished goods were ultimately shipped to the importer by the local firm in the neighbouring country. In one case it was a fully-owned facility, and in three acses the overseas production facility functioned as a joint venture approved by the Indian government. There was one unit owned by a joint family; in all other cases the relation between the Indian exporter and the local production facility was through managerial control. For all practical purposes, the local party was a sub-contractor with the difference that exports were made in his name from a country where quotas were not binding. The Indian firm did not have any ownership control over the local party. The arrangement between the two covered either a royalty based management contract or an informal managerial control through control on sales.

Only 13 per cent firms (twenty-three of the 177 firms) in the sample which provided detailed data had deployed this strategy to overcome quota barriers. Table 43 shows that eighteen of twenty-three firms were quota firms. Table 44 shows that quota firms utilised foreign production capacity of 215,499 pcs/annum as compared to

### Table 43

#### No. of Firms Using Foreign Production

|       | Quota | Non-quota | All |
|-------|-------|-----------|-----|
| Yes   | 18    | 5         | 23  |
| No    | 130   | 24        | 154 |
| (n)   | 148   | 29        | 177 |
| N.R.  | 0     | 0         | 0   |

### Table 44

#### Foreign Production Capacity Utilised (No. of pieces)

|       | Quota firms | Non-quota | All    |
|-------|-------------|-----------|--------|
| Mean  | 215499      | 431250    | 277142 |
| Min   | 10000       | 5000      | 5000   |
| Max   | 72500       | 900000    | 900000 |
| (n)   | 10          | 4         | 14     |
| N.R   | 8           | 1         | 9      |

431,250 pcs/annum in case of non-quota firms. The installed capacity in such foreign production facilities varied between a minimum of 5,000 pcs/firm/annum to a maximum of 9,00,000 pcs/firm. However, this capacity did not appear to be fully utilised. It is pertinent to point out that even five non-quota firms used this strategy to over-come quota barriers. By definition our non-quota firms exported quota items up to 60 per cent of their turnover.

The initial shift of production to Nepal seems to have been some-what arrested as Nepal is now under quota in the USA. Besides, many of the Indian firms faced problems of production coordination, delay in delivery and possible binding quotas in the future. Some of the firms attempting a foreign production strategy could not get off the ground. One Bombay firm reported that it had set up a factory with forty machines in Nepal but the production could not get off the ground. The same firm was successful in Sri Lanka where export orders had to be shifted to overcome binding quotas.

In many cases the linkage of the foreign production facility with the Indian firm is of a temporary nature. Only if the firm is unable to get quotas in India or quota prices become uneconomical are orders transferred to the foreign production facility with the full cooperation of importers. Foreign production strategy is being used mainly as a strategy of the last resort by firms employing this strategy.

The most frequently used foreign locations were Nepal (twelve firms), Sri Lanka (seven firms), Bangladesh (three firms), Mauritius (two firms), Indonesia, Caribbean and Pakistan (one firm each). One firm also reported use of a production facility in Hong Kong due to the initiative of an importer. Another small Delhi-based firm reported a manufacturing facility of 100 pcs/day in New York which was run by the brother of proprietors of the reporting quota firm. It appears to be clear that such a shift in production is the direct consequence of binding quotas. Had there been no binding quotas, there would have been no such shifts in production. It may be noted that the costs of shifting such production are relatively minor as the firm places increasing reliance on the decentralised sector for its own Indian production. The foreign production appears to be playing a supplementary role to the firms' Indian exports. However, internationalisation of production by firms appears to be a new trend in India. It is an area that requires in-depth research for the future.

The internationalisation of Indian apparel firms spurred by binding quotas has also been experienced by apparel exporters in Hong Kong. However, such internationalisation began quite early in Hong Kong's apparel industry as quota prices skyrocketed. One study suggested six stages of this internationalisation process (Lau and Chan, 1984). In *stage one* firms in Hong Kong experienced export-oriented growth targeted at low price segments of import markets over the 1950s and 1960s. In *stage two* in early 1970s, firms in Hong Kong began to shift production from low to middle price segments, children to adult items and quota to non-quota items. In *stage three*, with the MFA in effect, quota prices skyrocketed making Hong Kong FOB prices uncompetitive under fierce competition from South Korea and Taiwan. Large firms began to plan off-shore production to reduce manufacturing costs as well as gain larger quota access targeted at low price segments. In *stage four*, the domestic production shifted to the upper end of the market while off-shore production remained targeted at the lower segment. *Stage five* is associated with shortening of distribution channels, trade related marketing investments, and overseas marketing subsidiaries. It is also associated with greater marketing orientation, shift from own production to sub-contractors in Hong Kong. *Stage six* is identified by large apparel multinationals concentrating on marketing and international sourcing. Marketing activities include creating styles and fashion, developing customers and outlets. International sourcing includes deciding on the best production for each specific order and providing technical support for achieving quality production. During 1984 only a few firms in Hong Kong were found to be placed in this stage.

It is difficult to predict the pattern of the process of internationalisation in the case of Indian firms solely on the basis of Hong Kong's experience. Currently, only two phases of the internationalisation process have been observed in India.

The *first phase* is between 1965 and 1982 when export-oriented growth targeted at the lower end of western markets continued unabated. The *second phase* began in 1983 as quotas became partially binding in some markets. The emergence of quota premia in several countries/categories has spurred the internationalisation of Indian apparel firms. This phase is expected to continue into the 1990s. What, however, did not happen in India till 1988 was the upgrading of products and major diversification into non-quota items and destinations. It will be interesting to study the future course of internationalisation in this industry.

## SIZE, EXPORT ORIENTATION AND GROWTH

Hypothesis 10 of this study pertains to the relationship between the size of the firm and its growth while Hypothesis 11 relates export orientation to growth. We can examine these relations with the help of data collected in the survey of firms.

Survey data show that the share of small firms among growth firms is 56.43 per cent while their share among non-quota firms is 64.86 per cent. The calculated value of Z for these proportions comes to 0.947 when the total number of growth firms is 140 and that of non-growth firms thirty-seven. The difference in these proportions is statistically insignificant. On this basis it cannot be stated that *'large sized firms are more successful in maintaining their sales'*. (Maintaining of sales implies a growth over the reference period.) Hence, Hypothesis 10 is not proven. There is no clear-cut relation between large size and growth as had been hypothesized.

Sample data show the export orientation index of growth and non-growth firms. It can be seen that both growth and non-growth firms are highly export-oriented—exporting more than 92 per cent of their sales. The difference in export orientation of the two types of firms is statistically insignificant. Hence, Hypothesis 11, '*Highly export-oriented firms are more successful in maintaining their sales*' is not proven.

On the basis of the above analysis we can state that neither the firm's size nor its export orientation explains the growth of the firm under a quota regime.

# 8

# Firms Marketing Activity and Quotas

The impact of the quota regime on a firm depends, among other factors, upon the extent to which a firm is involved in international marketing. The level of a firm's involvement in international marketing can be indicated by an Export Orientation Index (EOI)[1]. This EOI varies between zero when there are no exports in both the terminal years of the reference period to 100, when the entire output is exported in both years. Table 45 shows the most striking feature of this industry. The average firm in the industry exports 97.5 per cent of its sales. Small as well as large firms, quota as well as non-quota firms export over 96.5 per cent of their sales. This high degree of export orientation is maintained by firms in all the three geographic regions. Standard deviation around the mean values is very small and there are no significant differences in EOI of different types of firms. The only conclusion that can be drawn here is that domestic demand is of no consideration in the marketing activity of these firms. They are almost entirely dependent on external demand and hence, the impact of the quota regime is bound to be considerable.

## PRODUCT SPECIALISATION

The Industry exhibits a narrow product specialisation which reflects

[1] EOI focuses on the export-oriented growth of a firm between the terminal years of a reference period (i.e., 1980 and 1986). It is calculated as a weighted

**Table 45**

*Export Orientation Index of Apparel Firms (1980–86)*

|  | Mean | Std.Dev. | Minimum | Maximum | NZO's | (n) | N.R. | Z |
|---|---|---|---|---|---|---|---|---|
| *REGION* | | | | | | | | |
| Delhi | 97.72 | 11.51 | 22.67 | 100.00 | 0.00 | 123.00 | 5.00 | 0.59 |
| Bombay | 95.14 | 19.50 | 0.00 | 100.00 | 1.00 | 27.00 | 3.00 | 1.00 |
| Madras | 99.59 | 1.59 | 93.83 | 100.00 | 0.00 | 15.00 | 4.00 | 0.88 |
| *Q/NQ Firms* | | | | | | | | |
| Quota | 97.10 | 13.78 | 0.00 | 100.00 | 1.00 | 137.00 | 11.00 | 1.02 |
| Non-Quota | 99.29 | 3.78 | 80.00 | 100.00 | 0.00 | 28.00 | 1.00 | |
| *G/NG Firms* | | | | | | | | |
| Growth | 98.86 | 9.12 | 0.00 | 100.00 | 1.00 | 130.00 | 10.00 | 1.43 |
| Non-Growth | 92.29 | 20.57 | 22.67 | 100.00 | 0.00 | 35.00 | 2.00 | |
| *Size* | | | | | | | | |
| Small | 96.53 | 15.39 | 0.00 | 100.00 | 1.00 | 97.00 | 6.00 | 1.00 |
| Large | 98.81 | 7.09 | 45.00 | 100.00 | 0.00 | 68.00 | 6.00 | |
| *All* | 97.47 | 12.67 | 0.00 | 100.00 | 1.00 | 165.00 | 12.00 | |

NZO's : No. of firms responding with a zero
(n) : No. of responding firms.
N.R. : No. of non-responding firms.
Z : Z test value for difference of means.

at the firm level as well. Almost every firm in the industry exports one or more of the top five items that dominate Indian exports, viz., blouses, shirts, dresses, skirts and trousers. Table 46 shows that during 1985, share of 'other than top five' items in a firm's total exports was a meagre 13.3 per cent while it was 13.5 per cent and 12.4 per cent for quota and non-quota firms respectively. This implies that on an average about 87 per cent of a firm's exports belonged to these top five items. It will be noted that there was hardly any change (only 0.91 per cent) in the reliance on 'other than top five' items between 1980 and 1985. This implies that on an average a firm's specialisation continued to be confined within these five items. Therefore, its ability to substitute production was quite limited. Theoretically, a firm can produce hundreds of apparel items entering into international trade. Yet, in practical business terms its experience and skills are confined to very limited product options. The quota regime seems to have made no appreciable difference on this narrow specialisation.

**Table 46**

*Change in other than top five items' share %*

| | All Firms | | Quota Firms | | Non-quota Firms | |
| | Change[*] | Share 85 | Change[*] | Share 85 | Change[*] | Share 85 |
|---|---|---|---|---|---|---|
| Mean | 0.91 | 13.3 | 0.67 | 13.5 | 1.93 | 12.4 |
| S. Dev | 3.87 | – | 2.37 | – | 7.55 | – |
| Min | −5 | 1 | −0.1 | 1 | −5 | 5 |
| Max | 29 | 60 | 9.25 | 60 | 29 | 20 |
| (n) | 85 | 28 | 69 | 23 | 16 | 5 |
| N.R. | 0 | – | 0 | 8 | 0 | 1 |

**Source :** Q 7B of Questionnaire Phase I.

[*] Change implies Share % 1985 minus Share % 1980.

A more precise index of such specialisation is the Product Concentration Index (PCI).[2] The index varies from 0 to 1. It is 1.0 if

average of the share of exports ($E_i$) in the firm's total sales ($S_i$). The weight for the initial year is half the weight in the later year.

[2] $PCI = \Sigma Z_i^2$ (i = 1,3; $Z_1 \geq Z_2 \geq Z_3$) where i refers to the top three export products of the firm and $Z_i$ the proportional share of the product in annual exports. In most industries product classification at the product item level is difficult

only one product is exported and decreases if more products are exported. Survey data showed that the average PCI was 0.47 in 1980 and has basically remained the same in 1986,' at 0.46. During 1980 there was no significant difference among any of types of firms categorised in this study except that PCI of firms based in Madras was significantly higher than that of firms in Delhi at 5 per cent level of significance. However, during 1986 even this difference had disappeared. Product concentration among Madras firms had declined from 0.74 to 0.58. It would be pertinent to note that there was no significant difference among quota and non-quota firms with regard to product concentration either in 1980 or 1986. Further a comparison of PCI values for firm types between the two terminal years of the reference period showed that there had been no significant difference in product concentration over the reference period. Contrary to expectations there was no significant variation in the PCI of either quota or non-quota firms. The result is that Hypothesis 9, i.e., 'Quotas tend to enhance market and/or product diversification among export firms' is not proven in so far as product concentration is concerned. Quotas do not tend to reduce product concentration among firms.

## NON-QUOTA SPECIALISATION

During unstructured discussion held with respondent firms it was found that whenever a firm felt an adverse impact of binding quotas, it tried to shift to an item where quotas were not yet binding (known as slow-moving items) or non-quota destinations. Such items were classified as non-quota items. Table 47 shows the shares of such non-quota products (quota and non-quota destinations). It was found that there was no change in average per cent share of such items for the sample taken as a whole. However, with respect to quota firms the share of such items had fallen from 26.78 to 16.6 per cent over 1980 to 1985. Among non-quota firms the reverse was true—the share of non-quota items rose from 63.66 per cent to 75.81 per cent showing that non-quota firms had placed increasing reliance on non-quota items. The same Table shows the absolute quantities of such non-quota items per firm. It will be observed that

---

(e.g. engineering goods) as thousands of items enter the export trade and product lines vary from firm to firm making comparability difficult. The apparel industry in India is one of few industries where a narrow specialisation makes PCI a meaningful index.

Table 47

*Change in Non-quota items (1980-85)*

| | Share% | | | | | | 00,000 pieces | | | | | |
| | Quota Firms | | Non-quota Firms | | All | | Quota Firms | | Non-quota Firms | | All | |
| | 1980 | 1985 | 1980 | 1985 | 1980 | 1985 | 1980 | 1985 | 1980 | 1985 | 1980 | 1985 |
|---|---|---|---|---|---|---|---|---|---|---|---|---|
| Mean | 26.78 | 16.6 | 63.66 | 75.81 | 35.73 | 35.17 | 0.88 | 0.23 | 3.44 | 7.54 | 1.75 | 2.99 |
| Min' | 5 | 1 | 30 | 50 | 5 | 1 | 0.20 | 0.04 | 0.60 | 0.20 | 0.20 | 0.04 |
| Max | 100 | 35 | 100 | 100 | 100 | 100 | 4.5 | 5.6 | 15 | 38.25 | 15 | 38.25 |
| (n) | 21 | 35 | 11 | 16 | 32 | 51 | 15 | 3.3 | 7 | 15 | 22 | 48 |
| N.R. | 12 | 0 | 3 | 0 | 15 | 0 | 19 | 3 | 7 | 1 | 26 | 4 |
| NZO | 36 | 34 | 2 | 0 | 38 | 34 | 35 | 33 | 2 | 0 | 37 | 33 |

**Source:** Q 77 and 8, Questionnaire.

**Note :** Share represents quantum % share in total exports; NQ items included NQ items in quota markets and all items to non-quota markets.

even though the share of such items for quota firms has fallen, the absolute quantum of non-quota items exported has marginally risen from 0.88 to 0.93 lakh pcs/firm. However, the increase is substantial for non-quota firms—from 3.44 to 7.54 lakh pcs/firm. The conclusion we can draw is inevitable, that quotas have produced a shift towards non-quota items/destination only among non-quota firms. Hypothesis 6: '*Marketing strategy of firms shifts from restrained categories/countries to quota free markets/products*', is proven only in so far as non-quota firms are concerned.

It does appear that as quota restrictions become binding, non-quota firms place increasing reliance on quota free markets and products in their marketing strategy. The policy implications that arise from testing Hypothesis 6 are that non-quota firms have a vital role in promoting exports of quota free items to both quota and non-quota destinations. These firms are more specialised in such products and market segments in terms of their marketing channels, product adaptation, and promotional activity. Non-quota firms are more familiar with segments of quota and non-quota markets where demand for Indian material, skills and products exists. At the firm level the visible and invisible costs of shifting from quota item markets may be high enough to deter quota firms from successfully changing their marketing strategy. Hence, non-quota firms appear to be more effective vehicles of promoting apparel exports. Non-quota items are, however, sold to quota as well as non-quota markets. Sample data also provided the share of such non-quota markets in the turnover of different types of firms. It is observed that the share of non-quota markets which was 34.8 per cent has declined to 28.8 per cent but the difference is not significant. Non-quota firms' share of non-quota markets was 56.9 per cent as compared to 25.5 per cent for quota firms in 1980 and this difference was significant at the 5 per cent level of significance. This difference also remained significant in 1986. This strengthens the inference that NQ firms can be more effective vehicles of export promotion.

## CLIENT SPECIALISATION

One can also view the differences in marketing characteristics of quota and non-quota firms in terms of the number of clients for such products. Foreign clients of an export firm refer to buyers of merchandise who perform the import marketing function. They are essential operators in the overseas marketing channel who transmit the merchandise to the point of retail sale. Except for large retailers like departmental and chain stores, most other retailers depend on importers and wholesalers for imported apparel. From discussions with the trade it is learnt that nine out of ten clients of Indian firms are such importers/wholesalers who order comparatively small quantities per style. On an average an apparel export firm was dealing with 7.47 clients in 1980 and this figure rose to 9.91 in 1986. As per the sample data average number of non-quota clients among firms dealing with such clients was 2.86 in 1980 which rose marginally to 3.81 in 1986. In 1980, 53 per cent of the firms (ninety-four firms) were not dealing with a single non-quota client while this share was as much as 46 per cent (eighty-two firms) in 1986. This shows only a marginal reliance on non-quota clients by the industry. Intra-industry comparisons showed that in 1980 firms operating in Delhi had larger number of non-quota clients than firms in Madras (at the 10 per cent level of significance) and the same was true for large-sized firms as compared to small firms (at the 5 per cent level of significance). However, these differences had disappeared in 1986. No significant differences are seen in the number of non-quota clients among quota as well as non-quota firms over the reference period. A comment that can be made here about non-quota clients is that non-quota firms are dealing with bigger and better market intermediaries in non-quota markets even though their number is the same as non-quota clients of quota firms. This is true because non-quota firms selling to Russia and Eastern Europe are dealing with only one client in a country. Other non-quota firms dealing with Japan, Australia, Switzerland and other non-quota markets also deal with small number of large clients. This point is relevent insofar as it emphasises the better capacity of non-quota firms as vehicles of apparel export promotion.

## MARKET SPECIALISATION

We now look at the export market concentration of these firms. The indicator used is the Export Market Concentration Index (EMCI)[3]

---

[3] EMCI is computed on the basis of proportional share of exports of the firm ($x_i$) to top five country markets in its total exports. It is represented by:
$\Sigma x_i^2$ ($i = 1,5$; $x_1 \geq x_2 \ldots \geq x_5$).

whose value varies between 1 and 0. EMCI is 1 when one country market accounts for 100 per cent of a firm's exports. Its value decreases as the equality in the share of its top five country markets approaches. A fall in value of EMCI would represent market diversification while an increase would represent market concentration. EMCI values were computed for the sample. The sample of all firms taken together shows an EMCI of 0.62 and 0.60 in 1980 and 1986 respectively, indicating that there is no change in the market concentration. Sample data show that there were no intra-industry variations in EMCI among any firm-types in 1980. The same is true for 1986 except for a comparison by size. Small firms showed an EMCI of 0.67 which was higher than 0.49 in case of large firms and this difference is significant at the 5 per cent level. Apart from this variation there is no other noticeable variation. There are also no changes in this ratio for any firm-type between 1980 and 1986. The inference that can be drawn here is that quotas do not tend to reduce market concentration ratios of export firms. Hence Hypothesis 9, i.e., *'Quotas tend to enhance market and/or product diversification among export firms'*, is not proven in so far as market diversification is concerned.

During discussions with respondents across the sample one clearly noticed that firms were attempting to diversify to non-quota markets. However, this was not reflected in data presented here as they pertain to the years 1980 and 1986. This is so because QRs were only partially binding during 1985 and 1986. The impact of QRs on product and market concentration of firms would become clear after quotas become binding for a longer time and over a larger number of markets during MFA-IV. The diversification had been notable for the firms whose substantial exports were directed to USA, Canada and Sweden. However, it was noted that firms which were dealing with larger retailer clients, department stores, chain-stores who were bulk importers could sustain their sales even under binding quotas in USA. This can be partly attributed to the fact that such importers had a larger capacity to absorb the impact of quota prices. It may also be noted here that a firm losing sales on account of quotas may not necessarily succeed in the diversification strategy. Fashion changes and shifts in consumer preference may play a critical role on the success of the attempted diversification. Between 1980 and 1986 most firms had attempted to enter non-quota markets like Japan, Australia, Switzerland, USSR, Hungary as well as quota markets having non-binding quotas. Many firms had succeeded in their market diversification strategy while some had failed.

Among firms dealing predominantly with EEC markets such a trend was not noticeable. This is due to the fact that binding quotas in most EEC markets have not been as frequent and severe as in case of USA, Canada and Sweden during MFA-III.

Another diversification strategy used by some of the firms was to enter the domestic market to compensate for adverse consequences in binding quota markets. In 1980 only four of the 177 firms had regular sales in the domestic market. All four were small quota firms based in Delhi and their domestic sale was 31.25 per cent of their turnover. By 1986 seven firms had entered the domestic market and this share had risen to 55.1 per cent. It was observed that only five firms had tried the domestication strategy with success. This strategy is particularly relevant in view of the fact that the apparel export industry is predominantly export-oriented and almost entire turnover is exported with only a few exceptions at the firm level. One firm in Delhi which had tried to enter the domestic market with branded gents shirt had failed despite one full year of marketing efforts. The failure was attributed to non-existence of organised marketing channels particularly at the wholesale level which could handle large quantities. Success in this strategy was achieved by some firms who have built up a network of retail stores. Such a strategy is investment intensive and involves fashion merchandising experience based on brand images which may be quite beyond the current competence of most firms in this industry. It is noteworthy to mention that all the firms that have been successful in the domestication strategy are small quota firms. These firms are affected by the impact of quotas and the use of this strategy is influenced by the quota environment.

## LOSS OF SALES

When a quota becomes binding, a firm dealing with customers in that country/category generally stops seeking orders for those items. The uncertainty of quota availability and daily fluctuations in quota prices work against acceptance of export orders. A firm which is unsure of quotas tends to refuse confirmation of contracts.

It was found that 81 per cent of the firms covered in first phase of the survey had to refuse export orders due to these reasons at one time or the other during the period of MFA-III. Such firms are both among quota and non-quota firms. However, there are some large-sized firms holding large PP quotas who may accept more orders than their quota holdings. This is done on the basis of confidence about being able to purchase quotas in the future. This may be particularly true while dealing with old and established clients. Once an order is accepted, the tendency of the firm is to honour its commitment as the importer is not really concerned about the non-availability of quota. An importer pre-sells the goods to his clients and inability of the exporter to honour his contract can snap business relations. Several firms stated that once orders were accepted they sometimes had to ship goods even at a loss to avoid losing clients. However, about two-thirds of the firms reported that they could not execute orders even after receipt of L/C due to non-availability of quotas.

An idea about the extent to which firms lost sales due to quotas can be had from the sample data. Forty-three quota firms had lost an average of 2,44,000 pcs. The number of non-quota firms was few (only six) yet they also lost an average of 4,52,000 pcs each. Many firms were unable to estimate their loss of sales. They stated that once quotas became scarce and their availability uncertain, they stopped pursuing import enquiries in the binding countries/categories. The negotiations did not mature into contracts, therefore, it was difficult to estimate the sales loss in specific quantities. In all, 56.6 per cent of the firms in the sample gave estimates of their sales lost. These firms had lost a total of 12.72 million pieces worth of export orders due to the impact of quotas during the period of MFA-III. Of this loss, quota firms lost orders worth Rs. 10.49 million pieces and the rest by non-quota firms. This gives us an average loss of 2,65,000 pcs/firm reporting such loss. Working on an average FOB price of Rs. 37.2 per garment[4] this works out to a loss in sales of Rs. 9.858 million/firm.

The loss of sales does occur and cancelled orders become the medium of transmitting scarcity signals that give rise to quota premia in one or more sectors of the export industry. It is true that some of the orders lost would go to firms holding PP quotas, yet

[4] Average price per piece on the basis of mean of average prices for 1983, 1984 and 1985.

quota premium would come into play hiking the FOB price of the products.

## FIRMS' RESPONSE TO CHANGES IN QUOTA REGIME

There are two distinct schools of thought on the possible consequences of abrogation of MFA and a return to the GATT regime. The pessimist school advocates the continuance of MFA, as without quotas, in its view, the market share of India and its exports could fall. The argument is based on the premise that Indian apparel exports are uncompetitive and quotas ensure protected market access. The optimist school advocates that removal of quotas would enhance Indian market share and exports as Indian apparel has a competitive edge in the cotton dominated sector. Respondents were asked to state their views on the possible consequence of (*a*) introduction of global quotas and (*b*) free trade without any quotas.

The responses are given in Table 48 which shows that 44 per cent of firms felt that their exports would go up under global import quotas as compared to 34 per cent who felt that their exports would decrease. Most respondents were unaware of the details of the MFA and considered quota allocations as a consequence of government policy. Global quotas were distinguished from MFA quotas by the fact that the former would be allocated in the importing country. This was perceived to give the import firm a stronger bargaining position as compared to the present system. Even in such a situation 19 per cent of the firms felt that a change to a global quota would not affect their business in any manner. It may be pointed out at this stage that there are well-entrenched vested interests in the export trade and industry that advocate the continuation of the current regime. They reflect the pessimist approach arguing that any shift to global quotas would adversely affect national export earnings.

Around 82.5 per cent respondents felt that they would stand to gain if quotas were abolished as compared to 9 per cent who felt that they would not gain. It may be mentioned that these responses of firms are based on their perception about firm-specific competitive advantages in their respective markets. An abolition of quotas in the importing country was perceived by the respondents as a return to the normal trading regime, i.e., a return to the GATT framework. For the firm it meant a capability to compete with competitors

Table 48

Possible impact of change in Quota regime: No of firms responding

| | In Case of Global Quotas | | | | In Case of No Quotas | | | |
|---|---|---|---|---|---|---|---|---|
| | Will go up | No effect | Will come down | NR | Will go up | No effect | Will come down | NR |
| All | 78.00 | 33.00 | 60.00 | 3.00 | 146.00 | 12.00 | 16.00 | 3.00 |
| *Region* | | | | | | | | |
| Delhi | 54.00 | 29.00 | 42.00 | 3.00 | 109.00 | 7.00 | 11.00 | 1.00 |
| Bombay | 12.00 | 3.00 | 13.00 | 0.00 | 21.00 | 4.00 | 5.00 | 0.00 |
| Madras | 12.00 | 1.00 | 5.00 | 0.00 | 16.00 | 1.00 | 0.00 | 2.00 |
| *Q/NQ firms* | | | | | | | | |
| Quota | 65.00 | 27.00 | 51.00 | 2.00 | 125.00 | 8.00 | 12.00 | 3.00 |
| Non-Quota | 13.00 | 6.00 | 9.00 | 1.00 | 21.00 | 4.00 | 4.00 | 0.00 |
| *G/NG Firms* | | | | | | | | |
| Growth | 58.00 | 27.00 | 52.00 | 2.00 | 115.00 | 8.00 | 15.00 | 2.00 |
| Non-Growth | 20.00 | 6.00 | 8.00 | 1.00 | 31.00 | 4.00 | 1.00 | 1.00 |
| *Size* | | | | | | | | |
| Small | 43.00 | 20.00 | 38.00 | 2.00 | 85.00 | 6.00 | 10.00 | 2.00 |
| Large | 35.00 | 13.00 | 22.00 | 1.00 | 61.00 | 6.00 | 6.00 | 1.00 |

**Note:** NR: No. of non-responding firms.

on an equal footing. Tariff barriers under the GATT regime would be non-discriminatory and be equally applicable to firms from all exporting countries. A large number of respondents who felt that their sales would decline under global quotas viewed a no-quota situation with optimism. Going by the perception of firms in this study one can say that Indian export trade and industry would feel better off under a no-quota regime even if importing countries were to raise their tariff barriers.

## NATURE OF COMPETITION

The firms were conscious of the nature and degree of competition they faced in their markets. Each firm specified its major competitors and Table 49 lists India's major competitors. Major competitors include Taiwan, Hong Kong, South Korea, Pakistan, China, Sri Lanka, Bangladesh and Nepal in almost every major apparel market. It may be noted that the product lines of China, Pakistan, Sri Lanka, Bangladesh and Nepal are directly competitive with Indian products. Taiwan, Hong Kong and South Korea are in the higher price garments and, therefore, direct competition is confined to only some market segments. On the whole the respondent firms struck an optimistic note of being able to meet such competition in the event MFA was abrogated.

Respondents admitted that exporters in South Korea, Taiwan, Hong Kong and China have an edge over Indian firms in basic and simple apparel which normally has bulk-sized orders. The Indian edge is in complicated tailored styles, embroidered, hand-crafted or ornamented styles using fine trimmings, cut work, tuckings, plaits, pin tucks, patchwork, sequins, etc., which consume a lot of artisan skills. Indian firms generally specialise in small production runs per style. Handloom and powerloom fabrics add to the competitive edge as small quantities can be produced to meet buyers' design and specifications. Particular mention can be made of yarn dyed fabrics (which have been made a special target for sub-ceilings in the 1986 Indo-US bilateral agreement), novelty fabrics, checks and stripes, dobbies, etc. In fact the Indian handloom and powerloom sector which supplies bulk of fabrics for apparel export has the flexibility of adapting to changes in fashion trends at short notice. This sector can supply 300 to 3,000 metres of fabrics in the same time and is the backbone of apparel exports as it can supply a wide variety of colours even in small quantities. The competitive edge is, however, confined to 100 per cent cotton apparel and the industry has little to offer for the winter markets.

Table 49

India's competitors in Apparel Market : no. of firms reporting competition

| Apparel Markets: | U.S.A. | | EEC | | Canada | | Sweden | | Austria | | Japan | | Hungary | |
|---|---|---|---|---|---|---|---|---|---|---|---|---|---|---|
| India's competitors | Q | NQ | Q | NQ | Q | NQ | Q | NQ | Q | NQ | Q | NQ | Q | NQ |
| Taiwan | 26 | 5 | 15 | 4 | 1 | 1 | 1 | 2 | 1 | 1 | 1 | 2 | 0 | 1 |
| Hong Kong | 24 | 3 | 15 | 3 | 4 | 1 | 1 | 1 | 1 | 1 | 1 | 2 | 0 | 3 |
| Bangladesh | 13 | 3 | 6 | 1 | 3 | 0 | 0 | 1 | 0 | 0 | 1 | 0 | 0 | 1 |
| Korea | 17 | 3 | 13 | 4 | 4 | 1 | 1 | 2 | 1 | 1 | 1 | 1 | 0 | 0 |
| Pakistan | 10 | 1 | 8 | 0 | 0 | 1 | 1 | 0 | 1 | 0 | 2 | 0 | 0 | 2 |
| China | 11 | 4 | 5 | 3 | 1 | 0 | 0 | 2 | 0 | 1 | 1 | 2 | 0 | 1 |
| Sri Lanka | 17 | 2 | 6 | 1 | 4 | 0 | 0 | | 1 | | 1 | | | |
| Nepal | 5 | 0 | 3 | 0 | 1 | 0 | 0 | | | | | | | |
| Singapore | 1 | 0 | 2 | 0 | 0 | 1 | 1 | | | | | | | |
| Japan | 2 | 1 | 0 | 0 | 0 | | | | | | | | | |
| Brazil | 1 | 1 | 0 | 0 | 0 | | | | | | | | | |
| Mauritius | 1 | 0 | 1 | 0 | 1 | | | | | | | | | |
| Turkey | 0 | 0 | 1 | 0 | 0 | | | | | | | | | |
| UK | 0 | 1 | 1 | 0 | 0 | | | | | | | | | |
| Thailand | 2 | 0 | 3 | 0 | 1 | | | | | | | | | |
| Indonesia | 3 | 0 | 0 | 0 | 1 | | | | | | | | | |
| Malaysia | 4 | 1 | 1 | 0 | 1 | | | | | | | | | |
| Spain | 2 | 1 | 0 | 0 | 1 | | | | | | | | | |
| Peru | 0 | 1 | 1 | 0 | 0 | | | | | | | | | |
| Portugal | 0 | 1 | 1 | 0 | 0 | | | | | | | | | |

Source : Q 20b Questionnaire Phase I.

# 9

# The Market For Quotas
# and Quota Prices

Almost the entire literature on the impact of QRs is confined to the study of quota rents. Quota prices have been used by macro-economists to compute the import tariff equivalents of exports subject to quotas. However, there is considerable controversy as to when and how quotas become binding. On this point the present study is quite clear. Quotas are seen to have become binding when an export firm has to refuse or cancel orders due to non-availability of quotas. The non-availability of quotas to a firm may be either due to exhaustion of the quota ceiling or a sub-ceiling of the type mentioned in chapters 3 and 4. Whatever the cause, a firm would not like to accept an export order without being sure of its ability to export the goods under a quota. As shown earlier (in the case of India), once quotas became scarce they became binding on one or more sectors of the industry. The exhaustion of the open section is the trigger that signals the beginning of a market for quotas.

As soon as the open section exhausts, firms generally tone down marketing efforts to secure orders in the affected country/category. Those holding PPQ/MQ limit their marketing efforts to the quota quantities held by them. Generally, the order-shipment cycle varies between thirty to ninety days. Export demand for apparel manifests itself through a firm contract between the export firm and an individual importer. The exporter would normally not order for purchase of fabrics unless he is assured of a quota certificate at the time of shipment. Therefore, it is crucial that he gets the quota at the time of confirmation of contract. If there is no quota available on the relevant date, the contract cannot be confirmed. If quotas become available even a few days later, the contract under question would be lost. Theoretically, the importer can go to any other firm for the same merchandise. However, in practical business terms this does not happen because exporter-importer relations are built over years of working together. They are based on mutual trust and appreciation of each other's working methods and standards of performance. An importer deals with a specific number of exporters on whom he has confidence. He would hesitate to shift suppliers too often. In such a situation when an importer needs the goods desperately as a result of demand derived from his customers in the market, he is willing to pay a higher price. His willingness to pay a higher price becomes the cause for quota rents. The exporter then seeks to buy quota from the PP quota holders on payment of a consideration. We now examine quota prices with reference to the situation in 1987 and before as compared to 1988, the year in which quota auctions were introduced for the first time.

## QUOTA PRICES PRIOR TO 1988

Quota rents arise only with respect to those products where restrictions became binding by exhaustion of the open quota section. It would be erroneous to assume that quotas are not binding below 100 per cent utilisation levels. It has been shown earlier that actual administration of quotas can make restrictions binding even at less than 100 per cent levels of utilisation. As soon as quotas become binding on the firm which has an export order, there emerges a market for sale and purchase of quotas. PP quota holders are sellers and holders of confirmed orders are buyers. Since PP quotas are allocated for a specific country/category, even firms holding PP quota enter the market as buyers. This may happen when the firm holds PP quotas in a category other than in which it has an export order.

Table 50 shows the country/categories causing quota rents at one time or the other during the period of MFA-III (1982 to 1986)

Table 50

*Country/Categories Under Binding Quota in India*
*(MFA-III and MFA-IV)*

| Country | Categories | |
| --- | --- | --- |
| | *MFA-III* | *MFA-IV (1987)* |
| USA | 335, 336, 339, 340, 341, 342, 347/48, 640, 641, 642. | 336, 337, 340, 341, 342, 345, 347/48, 378, 641, 642. |
| Canada | 2, 4 | 4 |
| Sweden | 2, 10 | 5, 9, 10 |
| France | 7, 26, 27,29 | 4, 6, 7, 8, 26, 27, 29 |
| U K | 4, 8, 26, 27, 29 | 6, 26, 27, 29 |
| West Germany | 4, 6, 7, 15-B, 26 27 | 4, 7, 8, 27, 29 |
| Italy | 7, 8, 26 | 7, 45 |
| Benelux | 8 | 4, 7, 8 |
| Ireland | | 7 |
| Denmark | | 4, 5, 7 |
| Norway | | 8 |

and MFA-IV (1987). These categories have been identified on the basis of discussions with firms covered in two phases of the survey.

Table 51 shows the range between which quota prices fluctuated during the periods when quotas were binding in the relevant country/categories. The prices are given per piece of apparel. It will be observed that the fluctuations were very wide. The price range shows the minimum and maximum prices of transfer of PP quota. The prices vary from day-to-day and are very volatile. In fact a network of quota brokers has emerged whose business is to arrange such transfers on a commission basis. Since the price consideration is mostly paid for in cash, it has become a source of generation of black money in the apparel industry. It is precisely for this reason that a majority of the firms interviewed were reluctant to give details on quota prices. Those who responded to the question spoke in general terms. Quota transfer is legal and is affected through the official Apparel Export Promotion Council. The transferer as well as the transferee file declarations with the AEPC but the transfer price is not required to be declared. In most cases the quota price is invisible to direct tax authorities as it does not reflect in the final accounts of most firms. It may be noted that this trade in quotas is entirely legal and the AEPC which is under the union government sanctions and gives effect to these transfers. These quota prices do not apply to all quantities exported by all firms but only to quantities that are affected by such quota transfers.

**Table 51**

*Quota Prices During MFA-III*

| Country | Category | Price Range (Rs.) | Country | Category | Price Range (Rs.) |
|---------|----------|-------------------|---------|----------|-------------------|
| USA | 335 | 2–18 | Canada | 1 | 10–40 |
| | 336 | 8–20 | | 2 | 6–20 |
| | 339 | 10–20 | | 4 | 6–14 |
| | 340 | 6–49 | | | |
| | 341 | 2–40 | U.K. | 4 | 0–6 |
| | 342 | 5–38 | | 8 | 0–2. |
| | 347/48 | 5–35 | | | |
| | 641 | 4–30 | Norway | 5 | 13–18 |
| West Germany | 4 | 2–6 | France | 7 | 4–12.50 |
| | 27 | 5–25 | | 27 | 7–20 |
| Sweden | 2 | 18–20 | Italy | 8 | 0–4 |
| | 10 | 15–16 | | | |

The second phase of the survey was conducted in 1987 by which time MFA-IV had begun. The quota prices which prevailed during early 1987 are given in Table 52. Quotas had become binding in a larger number of cases and the upper price limits in many cases were higher. Tables 51 and 52 are at best a reflection of black market prices during this period. No other record of price data is available. In both phases of survey it was noted that there was no single quota price. The price fluctuation was great.

Official quota administration has a lot to do with fluctuation of quota prices. A Bombay firm illustrated the impact of FCFS open section on quota prices: for the US category 641 during 1986 (II period) about 8,00,000 pcs were released on 1 May 1986 and were exhausted the same day. On 2 July 1986 another 1.5 million pcs were released and exhausted the same day. However, between 1 May and 1 July the scarcity position pushed up quota prices for this category, to Rs. 25 per piece. The secrecy or uncertainty in the release of FCFS quotas encourages such trading and the moment FCFS open section exhausts, quota trading begins.

**Table 52**

*Quota Prices During MFA-IV: 1987*

| Country | Category | Price Range (Rs.) | Country | Category | Price Range (Rs.) |
|---------|----------|-------------------|---------|----------|-------------------|
| USA | 336 | 2–38 | U.K. | 6 | 20 |
| | 337 | 20 | | 26 | 27–30 |
| | 340 | 8–35 | | 27 | 11–25 |
| | 341 | 8–60 | | 29 | 14 |
| | 342 | 10–36 | Norway | 8 | 25 |
| | 345 | 25–30 | France | 4 | 18 |
| | 347/48 | 18–20 | | 6 | 20 |
| | 378 | 25–30 | | 7 | 7–14 |
| | 641 | 6–32 | | 8 | 7–22 |
| | 642 | 5–6.50 | | 26 | 24–25 |
| West | 4 | 13–15 | | 27 | 20–30 |
| Germany | 7 | 6–25 | | 29 | 27–30 |
| | 8 | 3–10 | Italy | 7 | 6–8 |
| | 27 | 7–19 | | 45 | 15–20 |
| | 29 | 15–26 | Denmark | 7 | 13 |
| Sweden | 5 | 6 | | 45 | 30–32 |
| | 10 | 10–23 | Benelux | 7 | 7 |
| | 9 | 20–23 | | 4 | 13–18 |
| Canada | 4 | 10–20 | Ireland | 7 | 20–25 |
| | 21 | 20–25 | | | |

Additional quantities are not released by AEPC on the same day on the grounds that new applicants at a later date are likely to ship on higher cut-off prices. This, in the AEPC view, results in more foreign exchange for the country. The AEPC used the 'equity' argument till 1987 in holding that even after FCFS exhausts in a self-imposed quota sub-period, additional quantities should be released only on the first day of the next self-imposed quota period. It is argued that such time-based self-imposed distribution is equitable from the point of view of spacing out export shipments evenly over a quota period. This quota management device is also used on the ground that several bilateral agreements have anti-surge provisions under which the Indian side should avoid any sharp spurt in exports. It may be noted that this time-based distribution contributed quite a lot to fluctuations in quota prices prior to and during 1987.

## QUOTA PRICES IN 1988

Since January 1988 the government of India has modified the

the quota distribution policy. This change represents a significant departure from the policy followed till 1987. Under the 1988 policy a concept of auction of quotas has been introduced. The government has identified certain country/categories as 'superfast' and allowed quotas in these categories on auction. The system known as the Open Tender System (OTS) invites sealed bids from export firms for about 15 per cent of the total quantity available in a superfast category. A category is designated as 'superfast' if exports in that category have exceeded 91 per cent of the ceilings in each of the three preceding years. Undoubtedly, these categories represent quotas which bear the highest levels of quota rents. Auction of quotas is designed to allocate a part of quota rents for objects of public policy. The Government of India is not using this device to generate public revenue, rather it has set up an industry development fund to be used for apparel export promotion projects. The first auction generated Rs. 120.2 million for this fund. The government appears to have put only 15 per cent of the ceilings in superfast categories on auction as a measure of caution. The experiment has met with a roaring success and an avalanche of protest from some sections of the trade and industry. Powerful trade lobbies are at work for abolition of OTS but so far the government has been able to resist these pressures.

The Open Tender System (OTS) has thrown up interesting official data on quota prices. These prices are given in Tables 53 and 54 and fully corraborate the price data in Tables 51 and 52. Table 53 shows the auction prices of quotas for ten categories for USA. A comparison of these auction prices with the pre-auction prices in Tables 53 and 54 shows that in respect of five USA categories and two Canadian categories the prices were well within the price range for the earlier years. In the case of Sweden two categories (5 and 9) and Canadian category 4, prices in 1988 were in a much wider range than the earlier years. Table 54 shows that 1988 quota prices in eight EEC categories were in a wider price range as compared to earlier price ranges shown in Tables 51 and 52. These eight categories are West Germany (cat. 4), UK (cat. 4, 6 and 8), France (cat. 4), Benelux (cat. 4, 6 and 8). A widening of the price range represents a greater scarcity of quotas and a higher demand for those categories in the markets concerned.

These auctions have generated Rs. 120.2 million in January 1988, Rs. 77 million (June 1988) and Rs. 187.8 million (January 1989).

### Table 53

#### Ad Valorem Indian Export Tariff Equivalents
#### For MFA Protected Market: USA

| Category | Pn Mid-Price (Rs.) | Jan., 1988 | | Jun., 1988 | | Jan., 1989 | |
|---|---|---|---|---|---|---|---|
| | | Qn No.of Pcs. | ETEc | Qn No. of Pcs. | ETEc | Qn No.of Pcs. | ETEc |
| 335 WVN | 2.25 | 160482 | | 24548 | | | |
| (Women's | 7.25 | 2070 | | 5209 | | | |
| coats) | 12.25 | 13738 | | 3785 | | No | |
| | 52.25 | 0 | | 18 | | Auction | |
| Total | | 176290 | 4.57% | 80442 | 17.87% | | |
| 336 KT | 2.25 | 34206 | | 0 | | 39200 | |
| Dresses | 7.25 | 13190 | | 4000 | | 600 | |
| | 12.25 | 1200 | | 2000 | | 0 | |
| | 17.25 | 1350 | | 0 | | 675 | |
| | 22.25 | 2000 | | 0 | | 500 | |
| | 27.25 | 0 | | 0 | | 1610 | |
| | 32.25 | 0 | | 0 | | 1500 | |
| Total | | 51946 | 9.09% | 6000 | 16.52% | 44085 | 6.12% |
| 336 WVN | 2.25 | 0 | | 67480 | | 0 | |
| Dresses | 7.25 | 0 | | 42253 | | 0 | |
| | 12.25 | 0 | | 32282 | | 0 | |
| | 17.25 | 282541 | | 65688 | | 0 | |
| | 22.25 | 158463 | | 224808 | | 606439 | |
| | 27.25 | 1096 | | 97400 | | 297982 | |
| | 32.25 | 5980 | | 67618 | | 46191 | |
| | 37.25 | 0 | | 13861 | | 100 | |
| | 42.50 | 0 | | 55 | | 0 | |
| Total | | 448080 | 25.65% | 611445 | 28.87% | 950712 | 31.56% |
| 340 KT | 17.25 | 0 | | 0 | | 0 | |
| Men's Shirts | 22.25 | 134400 | | 0 | | 0 | |
| | 32.25 | 7500 | | 30000 | | 0 | |
| | 37.25 | 1000 | | 0 | | 0 | |
| | 42.25 | 1200 | | 0 | | 90000 | |
| Total | | 144100 | 52.36% | 30000 | 73.3% | 90000 | 88.02% |

*Table 53 (contd.)*

| Category | Pn Mid-Price (Rs.) | Jan., 1988 | | Jun., 1988 | | Jan., 1989 | |
|---|---|---|---|---|---|---|---|
| | | Qn No. of Pcs. | ETEc | Qn No. of Pcs. | ETEc | Qn No. of Pcs. | ETEc |
| 340 WVN | 17.25 | 658621 | | 0 | | 0 | |
| Men's | 22.25 | 488799 | | 0 | | 0 | |
| Shirts | 27.25 | 172900 | | 153020 | | 0 | |
| | 32.25 | 30000 | | 298095 | | 565107 | |
| | 37.25 | 0 | | 48000 | | 23395 | |
| | 42.25 | 0 | | 24760 | | 0 | |
| Total | | 1350320 | 34.45% | 523875 | 52.87% | 588502 | 50.7% |
| 341 MVN | 7.25 | 2616579 | | 2135603 | | 0 | |
| Blouses | 12.25 | 667724 | | 792500 | | 4868439 | |
| | 17.25 | 940 | | 5711 | | 123506 | |
| | 22.25 | 0 | | 0 | | 0 | |
| | 27.25 | 0 | | 0 | | 0 | |
| | 32.25 | 6235 | | 0 | | 3000 | |
| | 62.25 | 0 | | 1000 | | | |
| Total | | 3291478 | 18.48% | 2934814 | 19.20% | 4994945 | 24.8% |
| 342 KT | 2.25 | 0 | | 30000 | | 8200 | |
| Skirts | 7.25 | 0 | | 288 | | 24200 | |
| | 12.25 | 0 | | 1800 | | 12000 | |
| | 17.25 | 0 | | 0 | | 0 | |
| | 22.25 | 50000 | | 11260 | | 0 | |
| | 27.25 | 0 | | 720 | | 0 | |
| Total | | 50000 | 49.44% | 34068 | 9.09% | 44400 | 15.36% |
| 342 MVN | 2.25 | 0 | | 55000 | | 0 | |
| Skirts | 7.25 | 0 | | 168103 | | 650975 | |
| | 12.25 | 0 | | 117537 | | 200973 | |
| | 17.25 | 48001 | | 16619 | | 7350 | |
| | 22.25 | 271220 | | 5336 | | 1000 | |
| | 27.25 | 33003 | | 40 | | 0 | |
| | 32.25 | 12450 | | 0 | | 0 | |
| Total | | 364674 | 34.98% | 362635 | 11.98% | 860298 | 11.93% |
| 347/48 KT | 24.00 | 9174 | | | | 0 | |
| Trousers/ | 27.25 | 26670 | | | | 0 | |
| Shirts | 32.25 | 600 | | No | | 0 | |
| | 33.00 | 0 | | Auction | | 5700 | |
| | 42.50 | 0 | | | | 31720 | |
| Total | | 36444 | 85.53% | | | 37420 | 132.42% |

*Table 53 (contd.)*

| Category | Pn Mid-Price (Rs.) | Qn No.of Pcs. | ETEc | Qn No. of Pcs. | ETEc | Qn No.of Pcs. | ETEc |
|---|---|---|---|---|---|---|---|
| | | Jan., 1988 | | Jun., 1988 | | Jan., 1989 | |
| 347/48 WVN | 27.25 | 213511 | | | | 0 | |
| Trousers/ | 32.25 | 54740 | | | | 0 | |
| Shorts | 37.25 | 6000 | | | | 0 | |
| | 42.25 | 0 | | | | 364974 | |
| | 47.25 | 0 | | No Auction | | 22000 | |
| | 52.25 | 0 | | | | 4000 | |
| | 54.75 | 12000 | | | | 0 | |
| | 70.00 | 2288 | | | | 0 | |
| Total | | 288539 | 42.70% | | | 390974 | 60.90% |
| ETEm: USA | | | 25.53% | | 24.02% | | 28.95% |

**Note:**  No. of Categories

Gr. I: 9
Gr. II: 53

1988 Ceilings

78.823 million pcs.
.50    million sq. yds

## Table 54

### Quota Auction Price For EEC: 1988

*Price Range of Quota quantity sold under country/category to registered exporters in Open Tender System during first period 1988*

| Price Range (Rs.) | No. of Exporter Buyers | Qty. pcs sold under O.T.S. | Price Range (Rs.) | No. of Exporter Buyers | Qty. pcs sold under O.T.S. |
|---|---|---|---|---|---|
| *West Germany, Catg.4* | | | *United Kingdom, Catg.4* | | |
| 0–4.50 | – | – | 5.00–9.50 | 31 | 268000 |
| 5.00–9.50 | – | – | 10.00–14.50 | 8 | 47829 |
| 10.00–14.50 | 30 | 253832 | 25.00–29.50 | 1 | 5700 |
| 15.00–19.50 | 4 | 32268 | Total **knitted** | 40 | 321529 |
| Total **knitted** | 34 | 286100 | | | |
| *France, Catg.4* | | | *United Kingdom, Catg.6* | | |
| 0–4.50 | 1 | 1600 | | | |
| 5.00–9.50 | 12 | 79031 | 0–4.50 | 1 | 3600 |
| 10.00–14.50 | 15 | 79899 | 5.00–9.50 | – | – |
| 15.00–19.50 | – | – | 10.00–14.50 | 3 | 7560 |

*Table 54 (contd.)*

Price Range of Quota quantity sold under country/category to
registered exporters in Open Tender System during first period 1988

| Price Range (Rs.) | No. of Exporter Buyers | Qty. pcs sold under O.T.S. | Price Range (Rs.) | No. of Exporter Buyers | Qty. pcs sold under O.T.S. |
|---|---|---|---|---|---|
| 20.00–24.50 | 2 | 24,000 | 15.00–19.50 | 11 | 25,600 |
| 25.00–29.50 | 1 | 12,000 | 20.00–24.50 | 6 | 24,000 |
| Total **knitted** | 31 | 196,530 | 25.00–29.50 | 1 | 400 |
| | | | 30.00–34.50 | – | – |
| | | | 35.00–39.50 | 1 | 4,000 |
| *Benelux, Catg. 4* | | | Total **woven** | 23 | 65,160 |
| | | | | | |
| 0–4.50 | – | – | | | |
| 5.00–9.50 | 12 | 67,665 | *United Kingdom, Catg. 8* | | |
| 10.00–14.50 | 9 | 47,872 | | | |
| 15.00–19.50 | 1 | 3,000 | 0–4.50 | 13 | 57,744 |
| Total **knitted** | 22 | 118,537 | 5.00–9.50 | 79 | 611,323 |
| | | | 10.00–14.50 | 33 | 288,424 |
| *Benelux, Catg. 6* | | | 15.00–19.50 | 4 | 41,904 |
| | | | 70.00–74.50 | 1 | 5,250 |
| 0–4.50 | – | – | Total **woven** | 130 | 1004,645 |
| 5.00–9.50 | 7 | 22,000 | | | |
| 10.00–14.50 | 10 | 18,202 | *Ireland, Catg. 8* | | |
| 15.00–19.50 | 3 | 2,860 | | | |
| 20.00–24.50 | 1 | 216 | 0–4.50 | 2 | 2,400 |
| Total **woven** | 21 | 43,278 | 5.00–9.50 | 2 | 5,508 |
| | | | 10.00–14.50 | 4 | 16,000 |
| *Benelux, Catg. 8* | | | Total **woven** | 8 | 23908 |
| | | | | | |
| 0–4.50 | 4 | 11,440 | *Denmark, Catg. 29* | | |
| 5.00–9.50 | 23 | 139,404 | | | |
| 10.00–14.50 | 22 | 171,956 | 0–4.50 | 1 | 3,000 |
| 15.00–19.50 | 1 | 10,000 | 5.00–9.50 | 2 | 3,200 |
| Total **knitted** | 50 | 332,800 | 10.00–14.50 | 3 | 6,600 |
| | | | 15.00–19.50 | – | – |
| | | | 20.00–24.50 | 1 | 2,000 |
| *Greece, Catg. 27* | | | Total **woven** | 7 | 14,800 |
| 0–4.50 | – | – | | | |
| 5.00–9.50 | 1 | 480 | | | |
| Total **woven** | 1 | 480 | | | |

**Source:** Lok Sabha unstarred question no. 9141 dt. 29 April 1988.

These three auctions have netted a total of Rs. 385 million out of the rents accruing on the quotas. This, however, excludes rents generated on quotas that are not auctioned, but traded on the quota market which has been discussed in the preceding section.

These auctions have confirmed the view that since MFA quotas are broken down into fine product categories, quota prices relate to each given country/category. They vary from category to category, market to market and time to time. For instance there were ten separate quota categories auctioned for the MFA-protected US market. Tables 53 and 54 show that there were several price ranges at which different quantities were sold within a category. Not only did prices vary within a category but also from category to category and also auction to auction. The ad valorem export tariff equivalent varied from a minimum of 4.57 per cent in case of US category 335 (women's coats) in January 1988 to a maximum of 132.42 per cent in case of US category 347/48 (knitted trousers/shirts) in January 1989. Such variations in quota prices are found in respect of all MFA-protected markets. In case of Sweden five categories and in case of Canada ten categories were auctioned with a similar impact on quota prices. Apart from wide variations in quota prices the following points have also been observed:

1. The low unit value items bear a much higher export tariff equivalent than high unit value items, e.g., Indian knitwear has lower FOB prices than woven apparel. Indian knitwear exports bear a higher burden of quota prices. The same is true about children's garments as compared to adult wear. However, the computation in this study has been based on upset prices for adult wear only.

2. Different segments of the export industry experience varying levels of quota prices. For instance ETEc for export of T-Shirts to West Germany varied from 22.5 per cent to 64 per cent between January 1988 and January 1989. However, there were no auction prices for any other category as most German quotas were not binding at the export firm level during this period. Hence these equivalents are only applicable to categories subject to binding restrictions and not all export products.

3. The quota prices fluctuate and may even disappear in certain segments over time. This may be caused by fashion swings and changes in consumer preferences. Since India is no more than a

marginal exporter to the EC and US markets, even minor changes in fashion trends have a major impact and can make these quota prices disappear from season to season.

4. The quota auctions are confined to only about 15 per cent of the annual quota levels in the superfast categories. Export firms are allotted 85 per cent of quota levels without paying the quota price on basis of past performance.

   These firms display a tendency to bid higher prices to buy quotas. However, they are free to under-invoice shipments on past performance quotas so as to be able to comply with requirements of higher FOB export prices (upset price plus quota price) on auction quota shipments. So it would not be strange for customs officials in Europe to find one consignment being shipped by an Indian exporter to a European importer with two parts of the consignment shipped at significantly different FOB prices.

5. The tariff equivalents estimated for each MFA-protected market appear to be quite different from ad valorem export duties which are applicable to all quantities exported on an MFN basis. Hence, this basic distinction between MFN tariffs and tariff equivalents of VERs.

6. The highest incidence of ETE is borne by new firms entering the export industry. The firms that can profitably export after buying quotas in auctions are very efficient firms. However generally MFA quotas work as an entry barrier to new firms or established firms entering new quota bound markets. The MFA quotas not only freeze market shares of the supplying country but also freeze the structure of the export industry by providing disincentives to newer export firms. This happens as older firms are normally allocated quotas free of charge on basis of historical exports while new entrants have to buy the quotas for a price. This also works as an adverse consequence on the industrial development efforts in the developing-exporting country.

Table 55 shows ad valorem Export Tariff Equivalents (ETEm) estimated for each protected market. While they are designated as tariff equivalents, their incidence and impact have little in common with the well-known effects of a tariff. High tariff equivalents of over 25 per cent prevailed in the USA, France and the Republic of Ireland in January 1989. In January 1988 USA, Sweden, Benelux, UK, Germany, France and the Republic of Ireland exhibited tariff

## Table 55

### Indian Ad Valorem Export Tariff Equivalents (ETEm) for Each

| | | MFA Protected Market (% of upset price) | | |
| --- | --- | --- | --- | --- |
| | | Jan. 1988 | June 1988 | Jan. 1989 |
| | USA | 25.53 | 24.02 | 28.95 |
| | Sweden | 37.71 | 31.14 | 16.11 |
| | Canada | 17.45 | 7.42 | 12.86 |
| EC: | Benelux | 31.42 | 43.25 | 22.5 |
| | UK | 29.3 | 20.78 | 16.72 |
| | FRG | 64.05 | 55.55 | 22.54 |
| | France | 63.8 | nil | 40.65 |
| | Greece | 19.08 | 5.92 | nil |
| | Ireland | 25.22 | 38.33 | 34.5 |
| | Denmark | 10.49 | 6.24 | 11.1%. |

**Note:** For the year 1988 and January 1989, the quota auction prices are equivalent to quota rents for each individual category. These have been used to arrive at Export Tariff Equivalents for each country market as follows:

AdValorem ETE in each category: $ETEc = Pn.Qn \times 100/(Upset\ Price.\ Qn)$

Where: $Pn$ = Mid-point of the different price ranges for the quotas auctioned in each category.

$Qn$ = Number of pcs. sold in particular auction at each price range, Upset Price = Minimum FOB export price for each category
(excluding price paid for quota).

Ad Valorem ETE for particular Quota Market: $= ETEm = ETEc*Qc/Qc$ Where:

$ETEc$ = export tariff equivalent for each category of garment

$Qc$ = total no of pcs. sold in that cat. at different price ranges

$Qc = Qn$ for each category

equivalents (ETEm) of over 25 per cent. At this time the highest rates were in respect of France (63.8 per cent) and West Germany (64.05 per cent). The equivalents were considerably reduced in June 1988 for eight of the ten MFA-protected markets listed in the Table. This is attributed to seasonal changes in demand for Indian cotton apparel in the protected markets.

## TRADE POLICY IMPLICATIONS

Trade policy maximises welfare in the exporting country if quotas are auctioned so as to siphon quota rents from the export firms.

The auction provides a visible primary market for the sale and purchase of quotas. The re-sale of quotas by firms provides a secondary market for quotas, and tends, as in the case of India, to assume the features of a black market. As has been amply demonstrated by the Indian case, there are substantial revenues to be realised from such auctions without jeopardising foreign exchange earnings in any manner. The auctions also help to push up unit value realisation and provide ample funds for industrial development as well as export promotion activities. The auctioning of quotas allows free entry to new firms in the exporting industry, encourages competition as well as overall efficiency in the export industry. However, if only a small part of the quota is auctioned, it discriminates against the new entrants who have to pay a price for the quota while older exporters get quotas for 'free' on basis of historical exports. Hence, an optimal trade policy should allow for auctioning all quotas.

It has also been argued that quota rents can be appropriated by exporting country government by levy of export duties. The effects of such export duties would be highly uncertain due to two factors. Firstly, export duties would have to be levied on an MFN basis. Assuming ETEm provides an approximation of the tariff effect of the quota, a different tariff rate would be needed for each destination of export. This would violate the MFN principle and GATT obligations of the exporting country. Second, assuming that the GATT contracting parties permit discriminatory export duties on textiles and apparel as a natural consequence of MFA, they would be administratively inconvenient. They would not only tend to divert trade but also encourage trans-shipment via low duty destinations to high duty destinations.

## DOMESTIC MUNICIPAL LAW

The Indian attempt to auction quotas was successful but it met with a volley of protests from established export firms. Trade pleas to stop the auction were turned down by the government. However, export firms challenged the legal validity of the Government of India's decision to auction quotas. The Delhi High Court vide an order (All India Garment Export Common Cause Guild & Anr vs Union of India and ors. CWP No 3431/87, Chief Justice)

R.N. Pyne & D.P. Wadhwa) dated 22 February 1989 struck down the auction system as ultra vires the legal powers of the Government of India. The legal challenge was based on the powers of the government under the Imports and Exports Control Act, 1947, and Exports (Control) Order, 1988, issued under this Act. It was argued before the High Court that the government had no powers under the Act to impose a premium for sale of quota as it amounted to levying a tax on exports. Such a levy on exports violated article 19(1) (G) of the Indian constitution which provides to every citizen a fundamental right to trade. The union of India defended the auction terming the auction price as 'sort of licence fee' to be offered by the export firm to procure the quota. The petitioners contended that there was no licence required as export of apparel was under open general licence (OGL). The government could only oversee and regulate exports in terms of bilateral agreements with importing countries. Hence, the auction amounted to levying a tax without any law by parliament and thus was an unreasonable restriction on the fundamental right to carry on trade. The High Court held that the payment of auction price was a levy which was not authorised by any law and hence an unreasonable restriction on the petitioner's right to carry on trade. The court held that the government was carrying out the auction under its executive (not legislative) authority. Since such action operated to the prejudice of certain persons it must be supported by legislative authority. It was also held that the auction price paid was not a fee as the government was not rendering a service in lieu of the fee. Accordingly, as of April 1989, the auctions were suspended.

The government can resume auctions only if the Supreme Court of India suspends the operation of the High Court order or the Indian parliament exacts a new law authorising holding of future auctions. There is a good case for the Indian government to bring all quotas under auctions by means of a new legislation which can continue till the MFA is terminated. The trade policy rationale of auctions cannot be disputed. However, the domestic law must change itself to accommodate the situation created by deviation from the GATT regime.

## QUOTA TRADE

Nearly 72 per cent of the firms stated that they had bought or

sold quotas in the market. About 7.3 per cent refused to talk
about the subject and the remaining 21 per cent stated that they
did not buy or sell quotas. Table 56 shows that 73 per cent of
quota firms as well as 65.5 per cent of non-quota firms reported
buying/selling of quotas. It also shows that all types of firms in all
regions were engaged in the quota trade.

Table 56

*No. of Firms Reporting Sale/Purchase in Quota Market*

|  | NO | NR | YES |
|---|---|---|---|
| All firms | 37.00 | 13.00 | 127.00 |
| Delhi | 32.00 | 8.00 | 88.00 |
| Bombay | 2.00 | 3.00 | 25.00 |
| Madras | 3.00 | 2.00 | 14.00 |
| Quota | 29.00 | 11.00 | 108.00 |
| Non-quota | 8.00 | 2.00 | 19.00 |
| Growth | 26.0 | 10.00 | 104.00 |
| Non-Growth | 11.00 | 3.00 | 23.00 |
| Small | 31.00 | 8.00 | 64.00 |
| Large | 6.00 | 5.00 | 63.00 |

Sales/purchase of quotas was not a one shot activity but was
going on all the time. On an average a firm bought/sold quotas
about 4.7 times in a quota year. Sample data show that quota as
well as non-quota firms were engaged in this activity and there was
no significant difference in the number of times they bought/sold
quotas. It may be noted that about forty firms who entered into
such transactions refused to give details on the number of times they
bought or sold quotas. The only significant difference was by
size, as large firms bought/sold 6.15 times as compared to 3.46 times
in the case of small firms. This difference is significant at a one
per cent level.

The volume of trade in quotas was also found to be considerable.
Sample data show that on the average a firm bought or sold about
45,558 pieces during the reference period. The range of such transactions varied between 1,000 to 300,000 pieces per firm. In case
of quota firms the mean at 49,294 pieces was significantly higher
(at the 5 per cent level) than that of non-quota firms. This is so
because such transactions are vital to the business of quota firms.

Similarly, the mean in case of large firms was higher than in small firms, at a 1 per cent level of significance.

It was observed during interviews that low unit value items like cotton knitwear are affected adversely in this trading. This is so because quota prices bear a relation to higher value items and their absolute quota prices are quite high. Hence, exporters of cotton knitwear generally cannot afford to buy quotas in competition with woven apparel. Similarly, exporters of apparel for children are adversely affected. Another point that has emerged is that exporters holding PP quotas who do not sell in the market use their quotas to boost the sales of their slow-moving items. An exporter ties up sales of his slow-moving item with exports of an item under binding quota to an importer.

## IMPORTERS AND QUOTA PRICES

Respondent firms in the second phase of the survey were asked as to what share of the quota purchase price was normally borne by their importers. Only thirty-five firms gave specific data on this point. Table 57 shows that the average share of quota price paid by the importer was 53.9 per cent. There was no significant difference among any of the firm types in this respect. An inference that we can draw from these data is that for consignments where an exporter has to buy quotas, the importer bears about half the burden of the quota prices with the remainder being borne by the exporter whose profitability goes down. The enhancement in the FOB export prices on account of quotas would be equal to about half of the quota price for a given consignment. The windfall profits are made by export firms who do not have to buy quotas, yet they take advantage of the quota prices to extract higher FOB prices. It appears likely that the overall effect of binding quotas on FOB prices may be limited to a specific share of quota prices (about half in the instant case).

## THIRD PARTY EXPORTS

The disadvantage attached to the transfer of quotas is that the transferer loses his rights for PP quota in the subsequent quota year.

The transferee stands to gain as he becomes eligible for PP quotas in the subsequent period. PP quota firms having an eye to future quotas do not enter the market as sellers. They resort to another device called 'third party exports'. In such a transaction a firm having a confirmed export order enters into an arrangement with a PP quota holder. Under this arrangement the importer opens an L/C in favour of PP quota holder (who is a third party). The third party charges a price for allowing the export firm to use its PP quota. The goods are manufactured and shipped by the export firm but for customs purposes the shipper is the third party PP quota holder. In such a transaction the PP quota holder does not lose his PP quota for the future years. The PP quota holder being the legal shipper is entitled to domestic export incentives like duty drawback, import replenishment licences which may add upto 10 per cent of FOB value of such shipments. Because of these two benefits the price for such third party exports varies between 33 per cent to 60 per cent of the quota prices for outright transfer. More price information on these transactions is not available.

Table 57

*Importers Burden of Quota Prices*

| | Mean | Std. Dev. | Minimum | Maximum | NZO's | (n) | N.R. |
|---|---|---|---|---|---|---|---|
| *Region* | | | | | | | |
| Delhi | 53.91 | 24.07 | 2.00 | 100.00 | 27.00 | 35.00 | 66.00 |
| Bombay | – | – | – | – | 0.00 | 0.00 | 30.00 |
| Madras | – | – | – | – | 0.00 | 0.00 | 19.00 |
| *Q/NQ Firms* | | | | | | | |
| Quota | 52.73 | 24.55 | 2.00 | 100.00 | 22.00 | 30.00 | 96.00 |
| Non-Quota | 61.00 | 21.91 | 50.00 | 100.00 | 5.00 | 5.00 | 19.00 |
| *G/NG Firms* | | | | | | | |
| Growth | 53.03 | 23.65 | 2.00 | 100.00 | 21.00 | 32.00 | 87.00 |
| Non-Growth | 63.33 | 32.15 | 40.00 | 100.00 | 6.00 | 3.00 | 28.00 |
| *Size* | | | | | | | |
| Small | 55.71 | 25.58 | 2.00 | 100.00 | 19.00 | 24.00 | 60.00 |
| Large | 50.00 | 20.98 | 10.00 | 100.00 | 8.00 | 11.00 | 55.00 |
| *All* | 53.91 | 24.07 | 2.00 | 100.00 | 27.00 | 35.00 | 115.00 |

NZO's: No. of firms responding with a zero.
(n)    : No. of responding firms.
N.R.   : No. of non-responding firms.

However, prices for outright transfer and third party exports are quoted simultaneously on the quota market. Firms holding large PP quotas are withdrawing from entrepreneurial functions of production and marketing and earn profits simply by premiums on third party exports. Such firms advocate a ban on transfer of PP quotas so that they can be assured of quota rents through third party exports on a long term basis.

Two firms, a very large exporter and a public sector firm, stated that they did not use third party exports due to their company policy. The former did not use it because of negative post tax profitability, while the latter did not do so due to its corporate policy. Some firms said that there was considerable risk in such a method as sales proceeds were credited to the account of the third party and some firms had faced problems in dealing with strangers. Lately, firms were resorting to third party exports only where the third party was known well to the export firm. Some 63.3 per cent of the firms did not resort to third party exports due to these reasons.

Sample data also show that 36.7 per cent of all firms were using third party exports when they had to deal in binding country/categories. Sixty per cent of quota firms and 20.7 per cent of non-quota firms were resorting to such third party exports. While about 25.1 per cent exports of such quota firms were shipped by third party, this share among such non-quota firms was only 7 per cent. Quota firms were relying on such exports to a much larger extent than non-quota firms and this difference is significant at a 1 per cent level. Every firm which reported resort to third party exports stated that it had to do so only on account of quota problems. The share of third party exports was nil in 1980 because quotas were not even partially binding in 1980. It is quite clear that this device is a consequence of binding quotas.

## QUOTA EXCHANGE

Some firms prefer to avoid sale/purchase of quotas in which case they enter into exchange transactions. Two PP quota holders may exchange their quotas for a country/category required by them. The mutual exchange ratio is influenced by the prevailing market prices for quotas. A Bombay firm informed us that the exchange ratio for US quotas during second week of July 1986 was 2.1 pieces of category 341 in exchange for one piece of category 340. This corresponded roughly to the ratio of the prevailing quota prices for each of the two categories.

## QUOTA FRAUDS

Several export firms have been detected using improper quota documents to overcome severe problems caused by binding quotas or complex quota procedures. During MFA-III the government of India detected several cases of such quota frauds and criminally prosecuted scores of apparel exporters.[1] Many exporters have been de-registered on account of quota irregularities. Many of such 'frauds' took place. As quotas became binding for the first time, exporters were caught unaware with merchandise and without quotas. They resorted to tampering of documents, misdeclaration, etc., to ship their goods and avoid losses.

## PRODUCT UPGRADING

As mentioned in Part I, quotas are known to have induced upgrading. In order to discover the nature and extent to which Indian firms had upgraded their products, respondents were asked about the manner in which they had improved product quality. One parameter of quality upgrading considered relevant is better and more expensive fabric used (since fabric constitutes almost 54 per cent of FOB value of apparel). The other parameters are better workmanship in styling, finishing, tailoring and use of brands.

*Fabric Upgrading.* Sample data show the average increase in domestic price of cloth (in Rs. per metre) used for manufacture of apparel. It will be noted that there has been a mean increase of Rs. 4.9 per metre in the price of cloth used. The increase in case of quota firms is Rs. 4.83 as compared to Rs. 5.24 in case of non-quota firms. Almost all firms have reported such an increase. If price of the fabric is an indicator as to product quality, we cannot say that upgrading has taken place among quota firms. The increase in price of fabric cuts across quota and non-quota firms and may

---

[1] See Rajya Sabha unstarred questions Nos. 894 and 901, dated 26 March 1985.

be more likely the result of domestic inflation than quota induced upgrading.

*Quality Upgrading.* Sample data also show other dimensions of upgrading on the basis of responses of firms in the first phase of the survey. It shows that 83 per cent of firms have improved their finishing which enhances the shelf look of apparel. Some 85 per cent of quota and 75 per cent of non-quota firms have also reported improved finishing. Sixty-two per cent of firms have reported using better types of fabrics (not necessarily more expensive). The improvement in finishing is related to better quality control methods, installation of drycleaning and washing plants, usage of vacuum tables, fusing, buttonhole attachments on tailoring machines, etc. Better styling implies usage of trained designers (including foreign designers), shift to higher fashion segments or classic wear market. It also implies usage of handcrafting or embroidery in styling. Better fabrics imply usuage of fast colours in dyeing of fabrics, pre-shrunk fabrics, installation of machinery for printing and processing of fabrics. However, only very large firms were using imported fabrics as most firms found customs procedures for importing fabrics rather cumbersome. While both quota and non-quota firms have reported improvements in quality, it is not possible to infer that these improvements are induced by quotas. These improvements appear to be more as a result of the general maturation and accumulation of experience in the industry.

*Branding.* Apparel is a consumer product subject to fashion swings and invariably sold under brands. Brand preferences exercise strong influence on consumer behaviour and are used as a measure of product differentiation. One way of upgrading of products by exporters is the increased usage of exporters' brands or usage of brands in which the exporter has some proprietory rights. Sample data show that only 17.5 per cent (thirty-one) firms were exporting their own brands. Only twenty-two quota firms as compared to seven non-quota firms were using their own brands. Sample data show that on the average a firm using its own brand had been doing so far about 8.1 years. There is no significant difference in length of usage of brands between quota and non-quota firms. The range in case of non-quota firms is three to eleven years as compared to two to twenty-five years in case of quota firms. Non-quota firms appear to have longer experience in exporting branded products. Data provided by twenty-one such firms show that the mean number of pieces exported by quota firms under own brand is 42,577 pcs. (thirteen firms) as compared to 1.308 million pcs (eight firms) for non-quota firms. This shows that a comparatively small share of goods exported by quota firms is branded as compared to non-quota firms. Hence, there appears to be little evidence of product upgrading through branding amongst quota firms.

On this point it may be pertinent to mention that quota firms do not export unbranded products. Rather, almost every firm uses importers' brands. On the retail shelf they are sold as creations of particular brand names in which the export firms have no proprietory interest. It will not be wrong to state that most Indian apparel firms are working as sub-contractors for importers of apparel. In such cases it is relatively easy for an importer to switch sources of supply from India and to say Pakistan, Sri Lanka, Bangladesh or Nepal without adversely affecting his business.

*On the basis of the foregoing it cannot be said that quotas have induced any type of product upgrading.*

## UNCERTAINTY AND MUSHROOM GROWTH

The working of the quota policy till 1987 has thrown up an interesting aspect of the firms response to the quota regime. This aspect relates to the firms adjustment and response to the uncertainty generated by quotas. Firms not having PP quota were forced to produce goods much in advance of the date on which the open FCFS section began quota allotment. Since time allowed for FCFS shipments is only sixty days and was not sufficient for some firms, they took the risk of beginning the production process much before quota allotment. In case quotas were not available, the exporter would have to incur a loss either by buying quotas in the open market or by a distress sale of goods. This risk is accentuated because the local market for export quality apparel is almost non-existent due to differences in fashion, consumer preference and clothing habits.

This uncertainty and risk in categories where quotas became binding on the very first day of FCFS allotment had an impact on cut-off prices. Firms tended to quote high FOB prices in order to place themselves above the expected cut-off price. When every applicant was trying to do this, the cut-off price became very high.

This did not necessarily mean that foreign exchange realisation from FCFS quota shipments was high. Firms usually compensated the higher FOB prices by lower FOB prices on shipments going on PP quota or non-binding quota items. Higher FOB prices do not affect the buyer because the value of all his imports taken over a season are at agreed prices, which include the price impact of quotas.

It is in this climate of uncertainty that we should see the sharp increase in the number of registered exporters on the rolls of AEPC during MFA-III. The number of export firms on the rolls of AEPC was only 3,929 in early 1977 and by 1983 (i.e., in six years) only 224 firms had entered apparel exports. However, between 1983 and 1986 when quotas became binding for the first time in several country/categories, 4,809 firms entered the industry. Another 2,907 firms have entered the export industry between 1986 and 1988 as the number of registered apparel exporters on rolls of AEPC reached 11,149 on 30 June 1988. This sharp increase in the number of export firms is a direct consequence of binding quotas. PP quota holders were debarred from FCFS allocations until they had either surrendered their PP quota allotments or used a substantial part thereof. Since PP quota holders were shut-off from the open section, many of them floated new firms which were used for cornering of quotas on the open section. The AEPC reacted to this quota induced mushroom growth in firms by introducing an entry barrier against all new firms. For example, firms registered with AEPC later than 31 December 1983 were not eligible for FCFS quotas in 1986. For 1987 this date was 31 July 1984. The AEPC further tried to prevent such quota cornering by excluding associate concerns from FCFS quota allotment.[2] However, such quota cornering continues through associate concerns where such firms were not linked through ownership control but managerial control. Such associate concerns helped to maintain and increase business by cornering quotas. The manner in which firms have mushroomed is borne out by the fact that forty-seven registered firms are located at a single address and phone number in Bombay.[3] In less obvious instances it has been found that an export firm (which is dealing in a country/category where quotas have

---

[2] See para B (VIII) Garment Export Entitlement Policy 1986, Apparel Export Promotion Council, New Delhi, pp. 5, 20.

[3] AEPC Registration Nos. 8451 and 8497 in published list of members, 1986.

become binding in the past) has created such 'associate concerns'. In the present study 137 firms reported having such associate concerns and their mean number was 2.60 concerns per firm (see Table 58). There was no significant difference in this respect among quota and non-quota firms. Among quota firms the maximum number which a firm reported was fifteen and among non-quota firms it was nine. In some cases PP quota holders had created associate concerns by acquiring control of firms which were eligible for FCFS allotments. Even non-quota firms had such associate concerns due to their dealings in binding quota items.

### Table 58

#### No. of Associate Concerns

|  | Mean | Std. Dev. | Minimum | Maximum | NZO's | (n) | N.R. |
|---|---|---|---|---|---|---|---|
| *Region* | | | | | | | |
| Delhi | 2.27 | 2.08 | 1.00 | 15.00 | 0.00 | 99.00 | 29.00 |
| Bombay | 3.54 | 2.56 | 1.00 | 9.00 | 0.00 | 26.00 | 4.00 |
| Madras | 3.56 | 2.13 | 1.00 | 7.00 | 0.00 | 9.00 | 10.00 |
| *Q/NQ Firms* | | | | | | | |
| Quota | 2.62 | 2.22 | 1.00 | 15.00 | 0.00 | 110.00 | 38.00 |
| Non-Quota | 2.54 | 2.38 | 1.00 | 9.00 | 0.00 | 24.00 | 5.00 |
| *G/NG Firms* | | | | | | | |
| Growth | 2.77 | 2.37 | 1.00 | 15.00 | 0.00 | 111.00 | 29.00 |
| Non-Growth | 1.83 | 1.23 | 1.00 | 5.00 | 0.00 | 23.00 | 14.00 |
| *Size* | | | | | | | |
| Small | 1.80 | 1.33 | 1.00 | 8.00 | 0.00 | 79.00 | 24.00 |
| Large | 3.76 | 2.73 | 1.00 | 15.00 | 0.00 | 55.00 | 19.00 |
| *All* | 2.60 | 2.24 | 1.00 | 15.00 | 0.00 | 134.00 | 43.00 |

Note  : Mean includes reporting firm.
NZO's : No. of firms responding with a zero.
(n)    : No. of responding firms.
N.R.  : No. of non-responding firms.

The growth rates given to India under bilateral agreements negotiated under MFA are very small. Such growth rates eventually mean that the number of firms entering the export industry is restricted (as it is in the case of India) in order that existing firms can get market access. However, since the number of export firms interested in a country/category increases, the absolute PP quota share given to a firm stagnates. The intensity of the binding nature of the quota in such a country/category goes up. As binding quotas occur year after year, it becomes increasingly difficult for a firm to grow. So binding quotas not only raise an entry barrier for new export firms but also make it difficult for pre-existing export firms to grow.

# 10

# Direction for the Future and Conclusions

It will be worthwhile to focus on the policy implications of the findings in this study. This study as well its predecessor link study have thrown up interesting findings which suggest ways and means to enhance the long-term competitiveness of the export sector of the Indian apparel industry. However, before we present the findings on the behavioural response of the export firms to the quota regime, it will be necessary to specify the salient features of the export environment of this industry. Five salient features considered important are summarised below:

**I. The MFA**: The link study in Part I analyses the various developments that led to an increasingly protectionist framework under the first four extensions of the MFA. It notes that there are four undesirable features in the MFA, namely:

1. *Discrimination*: Based on derogation from the MFN clause of the GATT. About 55.8 per cent imports of apparel into developed market economies during 1980 were from exporting developed market economies themselves. The share of LDCs was only 38 per cent. Yet exports of apparel from developed market economies continue outside the MFA.

2. *Low Priced Imports and Market Disruption*: Even LDC firms exporting apparel in high price segments are subject to MFA restrictions for the only reason that they are located in LDCs. Moreover,

the low cost criterion is applied to OPT exports as well. Liberal treatment is given to OPT exports only to traditional OPT partners while shutting out newcomers.

3. *Unjustified Consumer Burden*: MFA has resulted in pushing up consumer prices of apparel in importing countries. Since consumer interests are not conscious and organised, there is not enough domestic pressure in importing countries against such high apparel prices. It has been estimated that if Sweden removes its QRs and tariff on apparel, it would result in a saving of SEK 800 per annum per household. Salaried families with children would save as much as SEK 1200 per annum. Sweden has taken a decision to opt out of MFA in 1991.

4. *Restriction Intensification*: The quantification of ceilings at the disaggregated product level many times results in quotas in areas where the exporter has no competitive advantage. Since there is rigidity in inter-country transfer or exchange among exporting countries and inflexibility in inter-category transfer, there is under- utilisation of quotas. This problem is compounded by self-imposed restrictions in exporting countries (as in the case of India).

However, with the extension of the MFA to its fourth term these undesirable features continue. It has been noted that the Indian efforts to bring textile trade under GATT have failed. Even a deadline for reverting to GATT by 1991 could not be included in the protocol of extension of the MFA to its fourth term. It is doubtful if MFA can be phased out by 2000 AD as a result of the Uruguay Round.

**II. Direction and Composition of Apparel Exports:** Apparel exports are the major textile foreign exchange earner for India today and hold promise for the future as well. Twenty-one out of 125 countries importing apparel account for over 95 per cent of Indian apparel exports. Of these twenty-one countries, sixteen impose QRs and constitute major markets for India. All these countries except Norway, Finland and Austria severely restricted Indian apparel exports due to QRs under MFA-III.

Exports of five items (blouses, shirts, dresses, skirts and trousers) constitute two-thirds of Indian exports to the sixteen quota countries. These five primary products constitute a very narrow product specialisation.

**III. Working of Quota Regime:** The working of the quota distribution system has shown that quotas have become restrictive even below category ceilings due to self-imposed restrictions not provided under the MFA or bilateral agreements. Quota distribution works to trigger quota premium in the open market and the quota administration encourages selling and buying of quotas in the open market. In the past quotas have become binding even below 100 per cent utilisation of a ceiling resulting in quota rents. The manner in which the quota market operates is explained in detail in Part I.

**IV.** *Competitiveness of the Apparel Industry*: It is based on four cornerstones:

1. Availability of a wide variety of cotton fabrics and tailoring materials;
2. Cheap skilled workers for simple cut, sew and finishing operations;
3. Structure of the trade and industry;
4. Product mix of the industry.

**V.** *Impact of Quotas on Export Prices*: The macroeconomic view of quotas has already been discussed in order to explain the emergence of quota rents as a consequence of MFA quotas. Findings of some western theorists are questioned on the basis of Indian experience of quotas under MFA-II and MFA-III.

Western macroeconomists have assumed that imposition of quotas actually leads to quota rents in all products under quota. This view is challenged. It is shown that quota rents in the exporting country occur only where restrictions actually bind the export firm. It is also shown that quota rents occur only in those country/categories where quotas bind the firm even below country ceilings. The severest restrictions are in the US quotas. It is estimated that Indian exporters earned Rs. 137.1 million, Rs. 574.17 million and Rs. 614.7 million during 1983, 1984 and 1985 respectively. Had the Indian government wanted, this could have been collected as export duty, tax or cess. These rents are, however, much lower than those prevailing in the Big-3 apparel exporters—South Korea, Hong Kong and Taiwan.

The impact of quotas on prices is a relatively lesser explored area. Quota rents may not affect export prices of all firms as restrictions are binding only for part of the year or when they affect only one sector of the industry.

## THE INTERNATIONAL TRADE AND INDIAN POLICY

The Multi-fibre Arrangement stands extended to its fourth term despite the opposition of LDCs such as India and Brazil. The efforts of

LDCs to phase out MFA have failed and the protocol of extension of MFA-IV does not even refer to a deadline for its phase-out. Observers of MFA-IV negotiations termed the LDC intiative of 1985–86 to phase-out MFA as a 'puny push' led by a 'timid or terrified band of loosely organised textile/clothing exporter nations' (Tuttle, 1987). The fourteen-page negotiating guide document issued by the GATT secretariat in June 1986 included only one page on 'Suggestions Relating to the Phase-out of the Existing Framework'. It suggested a phase-out by 31 July 1989. Rest of the thirteen pages listed specific quota tightening elements if the MFA was to stay. Observers felt that the LDCs advocating a phase-out 'failed to table well organised, well analysed and well articulated precepts for phase-out negotiation objectives'. It was even suggested that the 'phase-out agenda may have been articulated, controlled, and scuttled by several member states who secretly viewed their interests as being better served by yet another extension of the quota regime' (Tuttle, 1987). This view appears to be well founded when it is seen that alongside the phase-out efforts, individual LDCs were signing bilateral agreements. In fact two weeks before the expiry of MFA-III on 31 July 1986, Hong Kong renewed its bilateral agreement, accommodating US demands while South Korea was close to signing it. In the last two months of MFA-III, the EEC had entered into ten bilateral agreements (with the ASEAN five, Peru, Sri Lanka, Poland, Czechoslovakia and Columbia). These agreements produced a set of pressures in favour of MFA-IV. Another set of pressures was from smaller exporters which had assured market access that could be restricted due to larger suppliers after a phase-out (Jacobs, 1987).

Alongside the lack of commitment among LDCs to seek a phase-out of the MFA, there were and are severe protectionist pressures building up in the USA. The extension of MFA has not satisfied the US textile/apparel lobby. The Textile and Apparel Trade Enforcement Act of 1985 which was passed by both houses of the US Congress was vetoed by the US President in December 1985. Undaunted the US Congress set 6 August 1986 (six days after the expiry of MFA-III) to override the veto to coerce the US administration to negotiate a more restrictive MFA-IV. This move paid handsome dividends to counter MFA phase-out pressures within and outside USA. The US administration became over-cautious as support for this bill intensified and a more protectionist MFA emerged as a result of these pressures. The US textile/apparel lobby condemned the renewal of MFA as the attempt to override the US President's veto was lost short of eight votes of the two-thirds majority needed. This lobby vowed to renew its efforts for a more protectionist regime and returned to the 100th US Congress with the Textile and Apparel Trade Act of 1987. This bill sought to impose a global quota on all textile imports into the USA with an annual growth rate of 1 per cent. This bill was passed by the US House of Representatives in September 1987. By September 1988 this bill had also been passed in the US Senate by fifty-seven votes against thirty-two. According to a leading spokesman of the lobby supporting this bill, textile imports had continued to rise since the US President's veto of 1985. The continued growth in imports desired a policy to slow the growth which the 1987 Act (S. 549) sought to achieve. This bill envisaged global import quotas on 180 textile/apparel items at 1986 levels with an increase of 1 per cent per annum. This legislation was most likely to be vetoed by the US President as the Senate vote fell short by ten votes of a two-thirds majority to override a presidential veto. Nevertheless the forces supporting this legislation have re-surfaced after the new US President took office in 1989. Under this bill the US administration was given a number of options (Jenkins, 1987):

1. Choose to remain within the purview of the MFA
2. Terminate bilateral agreements and renegotiate them
3. Auction import quotas or issue licences up to limits of global quotas
4. Negotiate tariff reduction not below 90 per cent existing rates

The environment is less protectionist in the EEC as compared to the USA. The position of the EEC was liberal even at the time of the 1986 negotiations but it went along with the US in the final outcome of the MFA renewal. There are several interest groups in favour of the phase-out of the MFA in USA as well as the EEC. In the USA the groups[1] that are mobilising opinion against protectionist forces include trade associations of importers, retailers

---

[1] 1) AAEI-TAG: American Association of Exporters and Importers.
    2) RITAC: Retail Industry Trade Action Coalition.
    3) NRMA: National Retail Merchants Association.
    4) ARF: Amercian Retail Federation.
    5) CWT: Consumers For World Trade.

and consumer groups. However, the textile and apparel lobby[2] is well entrenched and the balance of power in USA is uneven (Giese and Lewin, 1987).

In such an environment a free trade regime with low tariffs appears unlikely in the near future. Two sets of alternatives to the MFA appear as likely. *First* a regime of global quotas which may be administered at the point of import. Such global quotas could either be auctioned or issued in the form of licences to importers. This could give freedom to the importer to import merchandise from the sources of his choice. Accompanied by broad banding of categories, such a regime could turn out to be more liberal than the present MFA as it would allow a greater degree of international competition. However, in such a regime a larger share of the quota rents could accrue at the importer's end. *Second*, a regime of return to GATT rules accompanied by higher import tariffs. Those tariffs could approximate the existing tariffs plus the tariff equivalent of quotas. Several studies have attempted to estimate tariff equivalents of quotas. One study found that 1980 rates of protection for sixteen garments varied from 24 per cent to 74 per cent with an average of 40 per cent. This was larger than the tariff which averaged at 25 per cent (Jenkins, 1980). The combined rate of protection for knitwear imports to Germany in 1981 was 70 per cent as against a tariff of 17 per cent (Cable, 1983). Another study estimated a quota equivalent between 2 per cent to 15 per cent on apparel imported to the UK in 1983 (Silberston, 1986). Our study has found the quota export tariff equivalent for Indian apparel exports to USA at 6.5 per cent, 24.5 per cent and 21.6 per cent in 1983, 1984 and 1985 respectively. However, these quota equivalents can vary from item to item, exporter to exporter, month to month or year to year. Yet, a set of figures can be worked out to keep bulk of the imports out of markets.

If India seeks a phase-out of the discriminatory MFA regime its apparel industry must arm itself for competition while its negotiators prepare a suitable negotiation agenda. The official policy on quota

[2] 1) ATMI: American Textile Manufacturers Institute.

2) AAMA: American Apparel Manufacturers Association.

3) Manmade Fibre Producers Association.

4) National Cotton Council.

5) ACTWU: Amalagamated Clothing and Textile Workers Union.

6) ILGWU International Ladies Garment Workers Union.

rents will be crucial for enhancing the competitive strength of the apparel export firms. Quota rents that have been appropriated by the Indian apparel firms since 1983 have and will continue to promote inefficiencies including the inefficient use of labour and materials. The low productivity levels of Indian labour will stagnate as firms earn profits from quota rents. Their costs and prices will become increasingly uncompetitive for a post-MFA competitive environment. As quota rents increase, domestic pressures for continuing MFA will also increase. Hence, the official policy should siphon the windfall profits from quota rents to maintain the competitive efficiency of firms. The OTS introduced in 1988 is a welcome step in the right direction but it falls short of the objective. OTS covers only 15 per cent of the annual levels of major rent-bearing categories. The quota rents on the remaining 85 per cent are still being appropriated by apparel firms. Official policy should work out a device to siphon out a part of the quota rents from all premium-bearing categories. This will enable apparel firms to overcome higher tariff barriers in a post-MFA regime. They would also be well placed to adjust to a regime of global quotas administered at the point of imports. If quota rents are not partly siphoned, it will be difficult for apparel exporters to overcome tariff barriers at rent-bearing cif prices they would have become accustomed to.

Indian negotiators must draw up a new strategy to seek a phase-out in the forthcoming MFA negotiations and the textiles negotiating group at the Uruguay Round. An organised stategic approach would require a reorganisation of exporting LDCs interested in a phase-out. This group of LDCs should conduct regular research, meetings, public relations as well as organise lobbying in the USA, EEC centres and Geneva. It should try to build a large consensus on a well-organised agenda framework for a phase-out regime. This group should seek out and solicit support from forces in the USA and the EEC which favour a dismantling of the MFA. The Indian government should take an initiative in this direction. The matter is a major agenda item at the Uruguay Round which have remained deadlocked till April 1991.

## QUOTA POLICY FRAMEWORK TO PREPARE FOR MFA PHASE-OUT

So long as quotas had not become binding at the firm level under

MFA-I and MFA-II, the administration of quotas was a matter relatively free from controversy. However, data presented in this study and its predecessor link study confirm that administration of binding quotas is not a simple routine matter. Hence, any quota administration policy in preparation for the phase-out of the MFA should seek to achieve three objectives, namely, siphoning of quota rents and minimising quota cornering; elimination of all self-imposed restrictions; and full utilisation of all quotas. To achieve these objectives the following suggestions are considered relevant:

1. Currently only 15 per cent of the annual levels in the superfast categories are put on the OTS. This share should be progressively increased over the next three years so that about half the levels in such categories are brought under the auction system.

2. Instead of releasing the entire quantity under OTS on the opening day, the OTS quantity should be released in at least four or five weekly auctions. These auctions will allow the quota prices to find their market level and allocate quotas to the more efficient firms in the industry.

3. All types of quotas (PP/ME/NQE/Public Sector) in the 'superfast' categories bear quota rents which result in windfall profit. A small part, say a fourth of the average quota prices in 'superfast' categories, should be siphoned-off. This could be done through a flat rate fee on allotment of quotas in each type of firms which are allotted such quotas for 'free' currently. This fee could be pre-determined on the basis of weighted average of quota prices for all quantities auctioned in the previous year. There is bound to be considerable resistance against such a policy measure in some sections of the trade and industry which will be forced to give up part of their unearned income or windfall profits. This, however, is imperative to maintain competitive efficiency of the apparel firms from a national point of view.

4. Quotas in binding categories should be freely transferable without any restrictions among all types of firms irrespective of the system under which they are allotted.

5. The official policy has already incorporated a suggestion to set up an export promotion fund from the revenues generated through siphoning of quota rents. The siphoning of quota rents is going to cause a strain on the financial liquidity of export firms. A part of these funds should be used to provide interest subsidy on funds blocked for purchase of quotas. It is suggested that funds required

for purchase of quotas should be covered under packing credit allowed by commercial banks at lower rates of interest. This could also be done through a credit arrangement to finance payment of fees or auction prices.

**6.** Floor prices should be based on firm level cost studies for average firms. In case floor prices are revised, the trade must be given at least six months' advance notice. Sudden changes in floor prices cause trade disruption which is undesirable.

**7.** All self-imposed restrictions which are not incorporated in bilateral agreements signed by the Government of India should be eliminated at the earliest. This applies particularly to sub-ceilings prescribed by the government in respect to products of a given type of sub-periods of a quota year. There is no logic in reserving quotas for one or more segments of the industry or for one or more self-imposed time-periods. Such sub-ceilings enhance the restrictive effect of the MFA. In case there is a surge in a given country/ category, it is for the importing country's government to call for consultations or enforce embargoes. It is only when the importing country asks for limiting a surge that time-period restrictions need to be put. Since Indian apparel exports are seasonal in nature due to cotton domination, it is possible to defend such a surge.

**8.** Quota allocation must be through a transparent system with every exporter having access to information on all aspects of quota policy. In the FCFS category, which needs to be retained and expanded, no exhaustion of limits should be allowed till the carry-forward provisions have been fully utilised.

**9.** Organised manufacturing should be accorded a more favourable place in the quota allocation policy. The 1988 quota policy shows a policy preference for manufacturer-exporters having a minimum of 100 machines and employing 150 workers. While the preference in favour of manufacturers is welcome, there is no rationale for giving a favourable treatment to firms employing over 100 machines. This study has shown that there are no economies of scale in this industry. Smaller firms are as efficient as large firms. Among the pre-existing 375 woven apparel manufacturers eligible for quota on 1 January 1988, 309 firms were having less than 100 machines or 150 eligible workers (Rajya Sabha, unstarred question 3814, dated 30 August 1988). Such a policy will eliminate a bulk of small-scale manufacturers. This policy will prove to be counter-productive and must be changed to accord the same status to all organised manufacturers irrespective of size.

## PRODUCTIVITY AND PATTERN OF PRODUCTION

In view of the absence of economic gains in labour productivity among mechanised units as compared to traditional units, and also in view of the internationally low productivity of Indian apparel workers, the following steps need to be taken to enhance productivity levels in the industry:

**A.** The decentralised manufacturing sector which undertakes about 79.3 per cent of apparel export production should be progressively brought into the organised manufacturing sector. The current pyramid structure with about 435 woven apparel manufacturers (recognised as of 1988 by the Textile Comissioner's office) needs to be modified in view of the realities. Fabricators having a permanent place of work and employing a core permanent staff should be enrolled as associate manufacturers by the Textile Commissioner and AEPC under a simplified procedure. These associate manufacturers along with the existing manufacturer-exporters should be given technical assistance to improve productivity which is more lucidly explained in the following paragraph.

The recognised manufacturer-exporters should be given a favourable treatment in quota allocations based on confirmed orders and existing capacity. The associate manufacturers should also be given some role in the quota policy to institutionalise their linkages with apparel exporters.

**B.** The AEPC and Textile Commissioner should conduct a census of fabricators having permanent facilities in order to enrol them as associate manufacturers. Such associates should also be given representation on the AEPC as well as be heard in any official policy formulation relating to the apparel industry.

**C.** The government should have a fresh look at the labour laws affecting this export-oriented industry. Due regard should be given to seasonal fluctuations in foreign demand and its low capital intensity in evolving fresh legislation to cover such an industry.

**D.** There is need to make a study of international comparisons in labour productivity in the apparel industry. This will pinpoint the manner in which Indian productivity can reach the levels attained by the big-three suppliers.

## PRODUCT DIVERSIFICATION

The export firms should be motivated to overcome narrow product specialisations. Such product diversification is necessary in order to improve market access at the firm level. The following steps can be taken:

**A.** Since the top five items constitute almost 87 per cent of the average firm's exports, the share of other items needs to be increased. The firm should be motivated to develop new fabrics and skills for products like coats and jackets; suits; gloves; rain-wear; uniforms and institutional clothing; playsuits and sunsuits; sports wear; gowns and housecoats; pyjamas and nightwear; underwears; sweaters; anoraks and parkas; socks and stockings; hats and caps; fur and leather apparels; and 'India items'.

**B.** Since the range of Indian fabrics available for such diversification is limited, exporters should be allowed to import fabrics at international prices for exports. The customs procedures for such duty free imports are cumbersome and hence the government should allow import of fabrics against REP licences and simplify existing duty free procedures for such imports. The procedures must be simple even if some imports leak into the domestic market. The benefits from such leaky imports far outweigh the costs thereof, if any.

**C.** The mill sector appears to have played a marginal role in supply of fabrics to the apparel export industry. This is quite true for small lots of fabrics requiring a colour variety. One way to integrate the mill sector with the apparel exports would be to allow excise duty free sale of fabrics to registered exporters. Such duty free fabric can be subject to lower rates of duty drawbacks. A similar system needs to be worked out for excise duty on processing, printing or dyeing of fabrics meant for export production.

**D.** Central and state governments should encourage domestication of apparel manufacturing firms. If a manufacturer has some domestic market, his ability to compete internationally is strengthened. He can engage in work all the year round even when foreign demand is low. A five-year domestic sales tax holiday for manufacturer-exporters who have no (or negligible) sales in the domestic market can help in this direction. If such a tax holiday is granted by the Union government and the states of Maharashtra, Tamil Nadu and the union territory of Delhi the purpose is likely to be achieved.

## SELECTIVITY IN EXPORT PROMOTION

There is no need to promote exports of products which are subject to binding quotas as they have become part of self-sustaining trade flows. Hence, export promotion of apparel in future should be on a selective basis. This selectivity can place a major reliance on non-quota firms as vehicles of export promotion. Firms which have a substantial share of non-quota items in a given base period should be given greater incentives in terms of cash assistance, grants for market development, etc. The existing system of support to the export of non-quota items/destinations should be made more selective in favour of non-quota firms which have demonstrated a greater tendency to diversify. In addition the following steps are worthy of attention:

**A.**    The exports of branded products should be encouraged as against unbranded or importer-brand products. Indian brands should be registered by firms in their overseas markets. Official support can be made available for registration of Indian brands under municipal laws of the foreign market. Exports of branded items should be given favoured treatment even in allotment of quotas.

**B.**    The provision of weighted deduction as export markets development allowance under section 35B of the Income Tax Act which was replaced in 1983 by turnover based allowance needs to be re-introduced. Personal selling expenses, overseas brand promotion activities and expenses on trade samples and participation in international trade fairs should be allowed a weighted deduction of 150 per cent for computing pre-tax profits. The maximum limit for such deductable promotional expenses allowed should be 10 per cent of export value of apparel or Rs. 1 million whichever is higher. This measure should be available to all registered exporters of apparel.

The current provision under the Income Tax Act providing tax exemption on export profits is an incentive only to established export firms that can generate export profits. It does not encourage firms to invest in developing new markets or new products as profits in such lines emerge only after a few years of market development. It does not encourage new export firms to spend on export promotion to penetrate overseas markets as export operations are relatively less profitable in the period of competitive penetration. The suggested export markets development allowance can be made available with the provision that an export firm may use one of the two provisions of its choice in an assessment year.

**C.**    Small exporting firms have been an important contributor to apparel exports. This study has shown evidence that export success is not linked to size. Hence, a case for special attention to small exporters. Market development by small firms involves expensive visits to new markets for cultivating new clients. Foreign travel costs can be subsidised up to 50 per cent to support first visits of small exporters to non-quota markets. Such a scheme can also cover the cost of bringing importers or designers to India to visit the exporters' establishments.

## TRAINING OF WORKERS

The long-term competitive advantage of Indian apparel firms depends on productivity of workers. The single-most important contributor to labour productivity is the training of different apparel workers. We have seen how the wage cost advantage is eroded by low productivity. Hence, any gains in productivity directly enhance competitiveness by improving the quality of production as well as product diversification and lowering of unit costs. The recently set up Indian Institute of Fashion Technology in New Delhi can be made to play a role in such training programme at four levels;

**A.**    Fashion and Design Capabilities: Training of designers, master-cutters and fashion coordinators in developing new styles matching with changing consumer preference. Use of computers in new design development, pattern-making and cutting are some areas for emphasis on training.

**B.**    Training of machine operators and product supervisors in workflow techniques, quality improvement methods, operation of power-operated machines, group production system, etc. This is particularly relevant for production skills for other than the top five items. This segment of training should focus on fabricators who are identified and enrolled as 'associated manufacturers' in the decentralised sector. Such training will be particularly relevant to firms who try to diversify their product line outside the narrow specialisation. Workers will have to be trained not only in operation of new types of machines, but also for efficient work methods on such new machines.

**C.**    Training of entrepreneurs and production managers in management techniques in plant layout, cost reduction, production scheduling, work study method, time measurement, purchase management, quality and stock control, etc.

**D.**    Training for support services: Specially designed training programmes would be required for master-dyers, producers of tailoring materials, master-weavers in handloom and powerloom sectors. Such programmes would improve the quality of various support services vital to the apparel trade.

These training programmes should be financed entirely from the funds realised by the AEPC from forfeited earnest money deposits and additional funds obtained from the siphoning of quota rents by the AEPC. Training programmes of the size and type suggested are well beyond the capacity of any single institution. They would have to be organised close to production centres as short-term programmes as well as in-company training programmes. Hence, private consultants should be shortlisted for assisting in the imparting of such training. There is no need to set up new institutions for this purpose. Rather, existing institutions like ITIs training centres, etc., in the central and state sectors in Bombay, Delhi and Madras can be involved in time bound projects by financial allocation for three to five years.

The importance of training of apparel workers may be gauged by the fact the Hong Kong provides for training of its apparel workers through the official Hong Kong Productivity Centre. This training is financed by a cess on export of apparel from Hong Kong.

The emerging trends in international competition indicate that technical developments in the USA are ushering in microelectronics based work systems. Usage of automated and semi-automated work stations will lead to lowering of costs in this industry (Mody and Wheeler, 1987). This competition can be met by enhancing productivity among Indian firms mainly through training of workers.

## OPT TRADE

So far none of the Indian bilateral agreements with importing countries have arrangements for Outward Processing Trade (OPT). OPT refers to assembling and processing of fabrics manufactured in the importing country in offshore facilities for eventual retail sale after re-import. India's largest apparel markets (US and EEC) allow for such arrangements to the advantage of a large section of their domestic trade and industry. Under US tariff schedules item 806.3 and 807, imports of such items pay duty only on the basis of foreign value added on re-entry into the US. US imports under item 807 have grown at an average annual rate of over 50 per cent during the 1970s. The share of apparel imports under item 807 has been growing over the 1980s and moreover, US apparel firms have used this facility to remain competitive in price sensitive segments of their markets. The bulk of the apparel imports under item 807 during 1970s were accounted for by Mexico, the Dominican Republic, Haiti, Costa Rica, the Philippines, Colombia and South Korea. It may be noted that protectionist sentiments against such imports are considerably lower since value added in the importing country is considerable. The Indian government should make serious efforts to include such OPT clauses in the Indian bilateral agreements and ensure that this trade, as and when it takes place, should be over and above existing quota ceilings as long as the MFA continues.

Such OPT arrangements are particularly important for markets like the USA where quotas have been binding during MFA-III and also continue to be binding under MFA-IV. Such OPT facilities will require considerable liberalisation of Indian import and customs procedures. Imports of fabrics under advance licensing and passbook scheme have become bogged down by bureaucratic delay and have not been popular. Simple, new procedures will have to be laid down if India has to enter the OPT arrangements.

Such trade will help in product diversification. In order to facilitate such trade, Indian firms will have to equip themselves with new types of imported machinery. Despite such machinery being under OGL, most exporters and fabricators have not imported such machines due to high capital costs. Import duties and higher unit cost for small orders push up investment costs quite beyond current levels prevailing in the industry. One way to reduce these costs is by import of such machines duty free or on nominal rates of duty. This is particularly relevant as India's competitors have access to such machinery at international prices.

## INTERNATIONALISATION OF FIRMS

Indian apparel export firms have begun to internationalise their operations as a result of binding quotas. Overseas investments in production and trade are likely to take place in the years to come. So far there is no official policy to promote such investment and internationalisation of firms in this industry. The government needs to study this area more closely and evolve a policy to guide and encourage overseas production and trade related investments by Indian firms in future.

# References

Arpan, De La Torre, Jose and B.Toyne. 1982. 'The US Apparel Industry'. College of Business Administration, Georgia State University, Research Monograph No. 88.

Cable, Vincent. 1983. *Protectionism and Industrial Decline*. London: Hodder and Stoughton.

De La Torre, Jose, M.J. Jedel, J.S. Arpan, E. W. Orgram and B.Toyne. 1978. 'Corporate Responses to Import Competition in the US Apparel Industry'. College of Business Administration, Georgia State University, Research Monograph No. 74.

Deardorff, Alan V., and Robert M. Stern. 1985. 'Methods of Measurement of Non-tariff Barriers'. Paper presented for joint UNCTAD-World Bank export group meeting on NTB's in Washington, D.C. July.

Englert, Michel. Undated. *The International Trade in Textiles: The Third Multifibre Agreement and the European Community*. Brussels: Bureau of Internations Europeranees.

Feenstra, R. 1984. 'Voluntary Export Restraint in U.S. Autos, 1980–81: Quality, Employment and Welfare Effects'. In R Baldwin and A Krueger (eds.), *The Structure and Evolution of Recent US Trade Policy*. Chicago: University of Chicago Press.

General Agreement on Trade and Tariffs. 1988. GATT Secretarial Document No. MTN. TNC/7 (MN). 9 December.

Giesse, Craig R. and Martine J. Lewin. 1987. 'The Multifibre Arrangement: Temporary Protection Runs Amuck'. *Law and Policy in International Business*, Vol. 19, No. 1.

Hamilton, Carl. 1984. 'Voluntary Export Restraints on Asia: Tariff Equivalents, Rents and Trade Barrier Formation'. Seminar Paper No. 276, Institute of International Economic Studies, Stockholm, April.

————. 1984. 'Economic Aspects of Voluntary Export Constraints'. Seminar Paper. No. 290, Institute of International Economic Studies, Stockholm, August.

————. 1984. ' Swedish Trade Restrictions on Textiles and Clothing'. *Skandinaviska Enskilda Banken Quaterly Review*, No. 4.

————. 1986. 'Restrictiveness and International Transmission of "New" Protectionism'. Seminar Paper No. 367, Institute of International Economic Studies, Stockholm, October.

Jackobs, Brenda A. 1987. 'Renewal and Expansion of the Multifibre Arrangement'. *Law and Policy in International Business*, Vol. 19, No. 1

Jenkins, Glenn P. 1980. *Costs and Consequences of the New Protectionism*. Ottawa: North-South Institute.

——————. (ed.) 1987. 'The Multifibre Arrangement: Its Shortcomings and Remedies'. *Law and Policy in International Business*, Vol. 19, No. 1.

Keesing, Donald B. and Martin Wolf. 1980. *Textiles Quotas Against Developing Countries*. London: Trade Policy Research Centre.

Khanna, S.R. 1985. 'Export Marketing of India's New Manufacturers'. Delhi: University of Delhi.

Kreinin, M.E. 1984. 'Wage Competitiveness in US Auto and Steel Industries'. Reprint Series No. 231, Institute for International Economic Studies, Stockholm.

Lau, H.F. and T.S. Chan. 'Internationalisation Process: The Case of Hong Kong Apparel Industry'. Department of Marketing and International Business, The Chinese University of Hong Kong.

Mody, Ashok and David Wheeler. 1987. 'Towards a Vanishing Middle: Competition in World Garment Industry.' *World Development*, Vol. 15, Nos. 10/11.

Tuttle, James C. 1987. 'Multifibre Arrangement Phaseout Prospects'. *Law and Policy in International Business*, Vol. 19, No. 1

Walter, Ingo (ed.). 1984. *Global Textile Industry*. London: George Allen and Unwin

Yoffie, David. 1983. *Power and Protectionism: Strategies of the Newly Industrialising Countries*. Columbia University Press.